Maybe I Should Just
SHUT UP
and
GO AWAY!

NEAL BOORTZ
"The Talkmaster"

The last no-holds-barred literary gasp
—part memoir and part commentary—
of a 42-year veteran talk radio
(A)Right-Wing Nut Job or
(B)Libertarian Icon

(Select one)

Carpenter's Son Publishing

Published by Carpenter's Son Publishing, Franklin, Tennessee

Edited by Cheryl Lewis

Cover Design by Kent Weakley

Interior Layout Design by Suzanne Lawing

Printed in the United States of America

978-0-9885931-1-4

PARTING SHOTS FROM FRIENDS...

I love Boortz, and I'm honored to call him a friend.

For the record: For all you Boortz fans out there, I tried many times to talk him out of retirement. While I was successful a few times in the past, I was unsuccessful this time.

Neal is an original both on air and in real life. He has the same sense of humor as that of a 15 year old going through puberty, which makes him fun, irreverent and just a great guy to be around. The airwaves will miss Neal's unique voice, keen intellect and patriotism.

Neal and I did not start out as best friends, but as competitors. With less than two years of professional radio experience, I was hired in 1992 to move from Huntsville, Alabama to go to Atlanta, Georgia to replace Neal on *WGST*—where he was already a legend in the marketplace. Lucky for me, Neal was serving a six-month non-compete period when I first went on the air. And when he did return to the air, on *WSB*, they placed him in an afternoon time slot while I was on in the mornings.

My new bride and I were headed out on our first week-long vacation one Friday afternoon and, as was my habit, I turned onto Neal's show at noon only to hear him mention my name. Not only mention my name—but start speaking to me DIRECTLY! Much changed at that moment—both for Neal and for me—but I'll let him tell you that story in this book. Let's just tell you about that vacation in words Neal would use: "It sucked." How did he know I was listening? He just knew. That's Neal.

When I returned from vacation, Neal's show had moved directly opposite mine, and I knew I was in a fight for my radio survival. Why? Because I was going up against the very best in talk radio. How did I know? I simply listened. I knew Neal was brilliant, funny, gifted and talented. I had to raise my game.

Then I discovered how hard he worked. Driving in one morning, I tuned into one of the most gifted radio newsmen in the business, Scott Slade on *WSB*. While I was listening, Boortz was in the studio getting ready. I was just headed to work… behind Neal already in show prep.

I was never behind, again. Every day thereafter, I would listen to Boortz talking to Slade at my DESK, not in the car. I was never going to let Boortz outwork me or run me out of town like he did to so many others before and after my time in Atlanta.

Neal's going to tell you some stories about our friendship in this book. If I don't like the way he tells them, well… I'll still be on the air and I can set the record straight. He'll be off in that BoortzBus thing of his, or his airplane, relaxing and living his well-deserved retirement.

Sean Hannity

***

So Boortz says to me, "You should tell women to stop farding in their cars while driving to enhance road safety." So I did. And was promptly cancelled on my Chicago affiliate, *WLS*, for 45 minutes. To fard (French) is to apply makeup to one's face. But no one heard the definition. Everyone thought I was being crude and vulgar. Who could have possibly thought that?

I don't know what else is in this book, but I doubt anything will top that, because nothing else in the book will be about me."

Rush Limbaugh

I am glad that Neal Boortz's "Happy Ending" retirement will not actually end. Listeners cannot afford to lose his insight, perspective and edginess. People who have never listened to Neal have missed an opportunity to challenge their thinking, which too many people don't even do, anymore.

Neal Boortz's impact on a lot of people and this country will never be adequately measured. It can only be subjectively surmised as "Wake up, people" before it's too late. Neal is an undeniable voice of reason.

Herman Cain

***

While driving in the mornings, I always try to tune in to Neal on the radio and, on many occasions, this outrageous man has gone over the top with his comments. Limitations? No way! Boundaries? No, sir! The result is remarks that are so clever, thought provoking and hysterically funny that I find myself laughing uncontrollably and I often have to pull off the road to avoid causing an accident. So, despite the productive life I try to live, and the philanthropy work I attempt to do each day, Neal has unknowingly come close to causing my demise. With Neal's retirement, I can look for many safer years on the road—but the ride will be boring, and certainly not as much fun. How we will miss him!

Bernie Marcus, Chairman
The Marcus Foundation
Co-founder, The Home Depot

DEDICATION

For my wife, Donna, and our daughter, Laura, with love, admiration and thanks for the years of enduring the endless stream of well-meaning people who began each and every conversation with "Did you hear what Neal said this morning?" No, they didn't. That would be because they never listened to me. That seemed to work out just fine.

CONTENTS

INTRODUCTION

Perhaps you know me—at least as a listener. Maybe you don't.

I'm a radio talk show host—or at least I was at the time I wrote and published this book. If you're reading it after the presidential inauguration on January 21, 2012, then I'm retired.

Yup. After 42 years, which let me tell you is a *whole* lot of days to be talking, filling the radio airwaves, I'm shutting up.

Sure, I may do audio commentaries on the Mothership—*News Talk WSB* in Atlanta—from time to time. I'll even fill in for other talk show hosts once in a while, and I'm sure to blog and continue writing irreverent little essays on current events and assorted nonsense at http://boortz.com.

Essentially, though, I'm retired. I'm on the road somewhere.

The travel bug hit.

Maybe I'll spend some time reading. Heck, perhaps I'll even re-read some of the other books I wrote. There are several, you know.

My first was *The Terrible Truth About Liberals*. After all, some things just need to be said.

Then, in 2005, Georgia Congressman John Linder and I collaborated to write *The FairTax Book*, published by Harper Collins. I had been studying and talking about the idea of replacing our income tax with a consumption tax for many years, as had Congressman Linder.

A group of economic researchers, funded by a $20 million stake from a group of Houston businessmen, developed an alternative tax system—a consumption tax that would replace all personal and business taxes.

That's right, business and personal income taxes, payroll taxes, estate taxes—all of them—and replace them with a national sales tax on retail purchases.

A focus group member involved in the research was heard to say "Why, that's a *fair* tax!" and the name stuck.

Congressman Linder and I merely intended to write the book, so that the details of this proposal would be available to researchers and anyone who would care to read it.

Then, *lightning struck!*

The FairTax Book debuted Number 1 on *The New York Times Bestseller List.* To this day, the book is still available in bookstores, and there are FairTax organizations in almost all of the 50 (or 57, if you are to believe our president) states. *(More information is available at www.FairTax.org.)*

I still believe the FairTax is a good idea but, as things stand now, it will never happen. Whenever enough people profit from a broken system, it will never be fixed.

In 2007, I wrote and Harper Collins published the book *Somebody's Gotta Say It.* The subtitle was *"Government schools, burning flags, and the war on the individual."*

It was, essentially, a collection of my rather articulate rants. (Yes, I say so myself.) No, this book didn't debut at Number 1. Seems some guy who wanted to become president had written something about audacity and hope and such things, so *Somebody's Gotta Say It* settled into the relative obscurity of Number 2.

Even while *Somebody's Gotta Say It* was realizing a great deal of success, *The FairTax Book* continued to draw attention. The Fair-Tax Act had been introduced in Congress with around 60 co-sponsors from both parties. Those who didn't want to see the massive reduction in government power that would come with the passage of The FairTax were fighting back with distortions and outright lies about this tax-reform plan.

So Linder and I reunited to write a book, *FairTax, The Truth,* which was published, again by Harper Collins, in 2008.

Now it's 2012 and it blows me away to realize that the career I've enjoyed most of my life is wrapping up. There is no narrative anywhere of what happened during those 42 years: the stories, the callers, the people I worked beside, the good, the bad, and the outrageous.

I have a granddaughter and love thinking that, someday, when she is a young woman, she might be curious about me and the life I've led. It hasn't always been pretty, but it has definitely been interesting!

So, before I shut up and go away, I want to share a few fun memories and insights (some not so fun). Let's see, we have dolphins killing tuna fishermen, throwing cats out of airplanes, being fired, being rehired, and finally making it to the National Radio Hall of Fame in Chicago. That one involves Rush Limbaugh.

I can't resist the temptation to get in my last licks on some political and social topics, so you'll find them here.

By the way, don't hold it against me, but I'm also an attorney. I retired from that miserable (for me, anyway) profession in 1992. The frightening thing is that, if I just managed to sit still for 14 hours of innocuous seminars—they call it "Continuing Legal Education"—I could write a check and put out my shingle and be back to practicing the next week.

You don't want me to do that. If I do, don't hire me as your attorney.

Trust me on this one.

If you buy this book, read through it, and then decide it hasn't been worth it, rest easy.

As with previous books, my royalties from the sale of this book will all go to my wife's charitable foundation. Yes, it's a qualified 501C(3) foundation, and I can't tell you how proud I am of the work she does and will do with your money.

Sure beats giving it to the government.

So… *here we go.* Enjoy!

Neal Boortz
The Talkmaster

SECTION I

THE TALK RADIO BUSINESS

Ever felt curious about the nitty gritty of the talk radio business? Some people succeed and some don't—and there's a reason. First, let me tell you how I got into this business in the first place—*instead of becoming a preacher!*

HOW IT ALL STARTED — AND WHY IT'S TIME TO STOP

I should prepare you—there's a suicide (not mine) involved in my humble beginnings as a talk radio host. Naturally, it couldn't just be boring, could it? But, first... [1]

We're going to do a rapid rewind here, so hang on tight. Remember? I want my granddaughter to know where I came from.

I was downloaded in Bryn Mawr, Pennsylvania in April of 1945. My father was a Marine Pilot, my mother a Navy Wave. Lots of people have asked where I lived while growing up, so let me share a few stopping points:

Philadelphia, Pennsylvania (origination point)

---

[1] Let's be brutally honest from the get go here. I'm really writing this for my grand-daughter. My history, such as it is, has never been put into writing before, and I want her to know where her Grandpa came from and how he got here. I truly don't think you'll be bored by this—it's an odd journey—but seems only fair that you know why I'm *really* writing this. Fact is, you're eavesdropping on a conversation years from now from a Grandpa to a grandbaby who became a young woman.

Thrall, Texas
Waikiki Beach, Hawaii
Laguna Beach, California
Hali Ewa, Hawaii
San Francisco, California
Newport Beach, California
Thrall, Texas
Virginia Beach, Virginia
Morehead City, North Carolina
Cherry Point Marine Corps Air Station, North Carolina
El Toro Marine Corps Air Station, California
Pensacola, Florida
College Station, Texas
Atlanta, Georgia
Naples, Florida
… and *still* on the go.

Crazy, right? It's the life of a Marine Brat—always new places to explore and new people to meet, but no lifelong friends.

Now think about that. Most of you, I dare say, have friends that date back to grade school, through high school and into college, then into your adult years. Me? Can't think of one.

Actually, I was supposed to be a preacher.

I know... *that's hard to believe.*

Yet that's what the pastor at St. Christopher's Episcopal Church in Pensacola, Florida thought. St. Christopher's was my church during my junior and senior years of high school.[2] I was the geeky little crew-cut kid with thick, black-framed glasses carrying the cross at the beginning of the procession then lighting and putting out candles on the altar.

I enjoyed taking stories from the Bible and reciting them at

---

[2]My first two years of high school were at Tustin Union High School in Orange County, California. My dad, a Marine pilot, was stationed at the nearby El Toro Marine Corps Air Station. Dad was transferred to the Pensacola Navy Air Station in 1961 and we moved my last two years to Pensacola High School. I graduated by the skin of my eye teeth in 1963.

church retreats and meetings and in Sunday school, using my own rather odd style. People seemed mildly entertained, and some involved with the church insisted that my future lay in the clergy, spinning these sermons from the pulpit on Sundays.

Close, but no cigar. I ended up spinning sermons, but not from a pulpit.

No, I never personally thought that being a preacher was my destiny. I was going to be an aerospace engineer. But there was that whole grade thing.

Know this: I was an absolutely lousy student—from first grade all the way through undergraduate school. I never made good grades. I was a pitiful student—because I was bored out of my mind. My grades were so hideous that, every single year on the last day of school, I would chew my nails to the quick, worrying about whether or not I was going to be promoted to the next grade. Yup, that bad. The only two things I can remember really motivating me during my government-education years were speech contests and the debate team.

I'm pretty sure I graduated from Pensacola High School with barely a "C" average. Government school—"C" average. Wow! You could certainly tell that I was on my way to some great things! That brings into question how I managed to get accepted into a college. I'm told that I made such an extraordinary grade on a college-entrance exam that my father was able to arrange my acceptance at Texas A&M University.

Let's not drag this education narrative out. I flunked out of A&M after the first semester of my sophomore year. Then, I pumped gas and cooked hamburgers for four months, until I managed to get back in for summer school to see if I could improve my learning skills. I did improve enough—mainly because it was a must—for A&M to welcome me back as a full-time student, lagging a few credits behind my classmates.

It was my "M.O." back then to blame circumstances and others for my lousy grades and study habits. My father, knowing I was somewhat of a slacker, had warned me that, if I flunked out of school, he was finished investing money in my education. He lived up to his word. From that point on, I had to work to come up with the money for tuition, a place to live, books, food and the basic incidentals.

So there I was, back in school with no way to pay for it. Student loans? What were those? At one point, I was getting up around 3:30 every morning to deliver about five different newspapers. From there, I would go unlock the doors at *WTAW-AM* and sign on as your friendly morning country DJ *Randy Neal*.[3]

So how did I become interested in radio? It was during my junior year at Pensacola High School. I was a new kid in town and knew absolutely *nobody*. Enter a government-school teacher who changed my life. His name was Roy Hyatt, and I don't even remember what subject he taught. I do remember, though, that they were looking for a student to read the morning announcements during homeroom, and he thought I had a nice voice. Would I like to try out?

YES!

So there you go—my first experience with the microphone. I would go to the administration office at the beginning of homeroom and read the announcements. Then, I would strut into my homeroom class like I was actually something. I wasn't, but I certainly strutted like I was.

This morning announcement thing started me thinking that I might want to become a disc jockey! Oh *yeah*! A pencil-necked geek with pimples, a crew cut, and thick glasses can be the school stud if he's a disc jockey, right?

I bought a little reel-to-reel portable tape recorder and started practicing. I would read a story from the newspaper, and then listen to it. Re-record and listen again. Then I would put records on my little RCA spindle-top 45-rpm record player and introduce them as they cycled through. Voila—disc jockey!

---

[3]My disc-jockey name, "Randy Neal", was prophetic—though I didn't know it at the time.

Girls galore! Here I come!

As it turned out, my dream of having a job on the air didn't come true until after I graduated high school—and then only because I was developing a skill for treachery. I was listening to a station in Pensacola when I heard the jock swear off mic. I called the station and told them I was with the FCC, and had just heard swear words over the air. I warned that I would be checking with them later to see what corrective action they had taken.

After waiting for about two hours, I called to ask them if there were any summer on-air jobs available.

"Why yes!" they said. "We just had an opening!"

BAM.

So there I was—an actual disc jockey—well, right up until I had to leave for Texas A&M. The first song I ever played on the air was Percy Faith's *"Theme from A Summer Place."* Boortz trivia.

OK, so where were we? Oh yeah. My father had cut off my education funding, and I was working every job I could find to cover the costs of continuing at A&M.

Throughout my life, the way to get me to rise up and actually do something was to tell me that I couldn't. I first realized this in my freshman year at Tustin Union High School in Southern California. I tried out for the swimming team and worked my tail off but, when the Tustin Tiller team traveled to our first swim meet, Coach Moon didn't assign an event for me to swim.

On the bus traveling back to Tustin, he told me that, even though I had worked hard, I just wasn't good enough to swim competitively. As consolation, he asked me if I wanted to be the team manager.

Huh?

So I bargained. I told him that I would do that if he would (a) allow me to continue to work out with the team, and (b) give me at least one chance to swim in an event at our next swim meet. He agreed. The next swim meet was against our arch-rival, LaBrea, and Coach Moon assigned me to the 200-yard freestyle.

Let's cut to the chase here: At the sound of the starter's gun, I hit the water, swam like I was being chased by a shark, and was already sitting on the edge of the pool when the second guy got there.

Take that!

From that point on, until I left Tustin High after my sophomore year, I never lost a race.

So much for being the team manager.

When my father told me I wouldn't be able to work and earn enough money to continue at Texas A&M, he suggested that perhaps I should consider the Pensacola Junior College (a/k/a The University of North Ninth Avenue). That was all he needed to say. It was Coach Moon telling me once more that I wasn't good enough to make the team.

And, so, I worked my own way through school. After my morning show at *WTAW*, it was off to classes.

When my last class wrapped up each day, I would hit some Bryan or College Station neighborhood to sell Fuller Brushes door to door. *Yes!* I was one of those legendary Fuller Brush Men. I can still remember some of the tricks of the trade. Wanna hear 'em?

My favorite was to knock on the door with a rag and can of foam cleaner ready. As the lady opened the door, I would spray this gunk on the door frame and wipe a spot clean with the rag. More often than not, the lady would at least buy a can of the cleaner, simply because she needed to clean the rest of her door. I also sold an aerosol can of something called Rich Puff Hand Cream. My pitch was that there was enough in that can to fill a bathtub. One lady made me prove it—and I did.

Oh, and are you ready for this old joke? One time, a lady opened the door in her negligee. At the time, I thought that was a rather odd place to have a door.

Ba dum pum.

Sorry.

Still my day was not done. After knocking on doors for hours, I put away my sample case and headed to Coach Norton's Pancake House to wait tables. When the last customer left, it was time for some studying (yeah, right!) and some sleep—until the morning batch of papers and a box of rubber bands were dropped on my doorstep.

Oh geez. Another story just occurred to me, so here goes:

My career waiting tables ended up at the Ramada Inn restaurant—right there at the corner of Texas Avenue and University, for you Aggie types. That place was being run by a true oddball, who would hook the waiters up to a polygraph every week to make sure we weren't eating biscuits or stealing his food. The whole place was blown up a few years ago; actually, imploded is more accurate. There's no doubt about it—thanks to that day, College Station is even more beautiful.

My final night at the Ramada Inn was the Senior Boot Dance. This was the prom, so to speak, for seniors in the Corps of Cadets. They would show up in their dress uniforms wearing their senior boots, and their dates would be wearing the most revealing and alluring dresses they could find. As fortune would have it, I was waiting on a senior with a particularly well-endowed date in an equally revealing dress. I couldn't help but admire the detail work that the seamstress had included in the low and open neckline.

The senior—a rather large senior, I might add—ordered one of those Mexican dinners that are served on a sizzling hot metal plate nestled in a wooden tray. Madam Mammary was adjusting herself as I approached their table with the food. At just the wrong time, someone pushed back a chair. I wasn't paying attention—not to that chair, anyway—and I tripped.

The aforementioned sizzling-hot plate slid off the wooden tray and sailed like a Frisbee straight down the front of that lady's dress. Here is where I showed the quick thinking for which I have become famous. *Did I mention the plate was hot?* I grabbed a pitcher of ice water from the adjoining stand, poured it down the front of her dress, and then raced out the back door of the kitchen.

I never even went back to get my tip.

Yes, the statute of limitations has been my friend for many, many years.

Perhaps you noticed a lack of study time in the mix of all these jobs and misadventures. True, but I did manage to hang on until the end of what should have been the finale of my last (senior) year. Being fired at *WTAW* actually gave me more time to study—not that I necessarily used that time for studying.

Wait, did I say "fired?" Yeah—*fired.* And it certainly wasn't going to be the last time, as you will soon learn.

At *WTAW*, it was that tarantula incident.

Got your attention?

Texas, you see, has periodic massive tarantula migrations. During one of these migrations, I managed to go out and collect about 100 tarantulas in a large cardboard box. These were to be used to screw around with the Saturday morning crew at *WTAW*.

Let me set the stage here: *WTAW* would sign off around midnight and sign back on the air at 5 in the morning. Oddly, the power switch for the studio was located under the disc jockey's console. You would have to sit in the chair and literally kick the switch to turn the place—lights and all—on or off.

And so it came to pass on one Friday night that I sneaked into the station after midnight and turned 100 tarantulas loose in the darkened studio. *100!* Don't worry. These suckers would bite, but they weren't poisonous—or so I was told.

The Saturday morning DJ came to work at the appointed time and walked into the dark studio. He noticed a crunch when he sat down in the chair. Reaching his foot under the console to hit the power switch, he illuminated the room.

Showtime.

Seconds later, he went screaming out the front door of the station. There were tarantulas *everywhere*. Crushed tarantulas on the seat. Tarantulas on the turntables, on the tape machines—tarantulas wherever you could put a tarantula. What's more, there was no doubt who brought them. My tarantula collection was well known.

It took well into the afternoon for the exterminating company to de-tarantula the studio. It took a good deal less time than that for the word to get to me that I was fired.

Ah, well. At least I was about to graduate.

So, why leave Texas A&M with just a few hours lacking before I earned a degree? Let's just blame that on a rather unpleasant case of domestic in-tranquility. You see, somewhere on the road of academic mediocrity, I decided that it would be a good idea to get married. The disc-jockey part of my workday had led to an introduction to a lovely little raven-haired Louisiana Cajun.

When my parents and virtually everyone that I knew told me they thought getting hitched was a bad idea for me, the idea naturally became irresistible. So... we got married.

Maybe our wedding night should have been a warning. Not her fault, mind you, but the hotel at Six Flags Over Texas (hey, the budget was tight) had this little coin-operated thingy on the nightstand. You put in a quarter and the bed vibrated.

I thought this would be pretty cool, so I fed it some quarters. Well, it wouldn't turn off. In fact, hours later, it still wouldn't turn off. I had to climb under the bed to find the plug, and got stuck.

True story.

Things went downhill from there. My brother thought it would be a good idea to use liquid shoe polish to put the "Just Married" signs on the bride's white Mustang. It wouldn't come off, so the car had to be repainted. Plus, her little poodle wasn't house trained and left unwelcome presents all over the apartment.

Let's just say it was not a good scene from the start. Nobody's fault—just a big mistake.

So, on the morning of July 1, 1967—just before I was to begin the summer semester to complete my degree requirements—I said adios and boarded a Greyhound bus, instead.

Destination: *Atlanta.*

Why there? No particular reason, other than my parents were living there at the time and the second Battle of New Orleans was underway in my Boortz College Station household.

During my great escape away from there, the bus made a stop in New Orleans and, to my delight, I discovered I was old enough to drink. So, it was an enthusiastic toast—or two—to the Cajun and back on the road.

I stepped off of that bus in downtown Atlanta on Sunday, July 2, 1967—and that's when the fun REALLY began.[4]

My first exciting employment? Well, let's see: I started out as the assistant buyer of fine jewelry at Rich's Department Store (now Macy's). Actually, I did have a memorable moment there that remains special to me. Just one, mind you, but it's a doozy:

One evening, as I was working the counter, Dr. Martin Luther King Jr. came in to buy something nice for his wife. I really didn't know then that this would be my first touch with greatness, but I feel privileged to have met the man.

My transfer to assistant buyer in Rich's carpeting department was less memorable. I finally left Rich's and, through random introductions, moved on to sell industrial chemicals on the road, work for an employment agency, load trucks overnight at a freight depot, handle the night-auditor duties at a downtown motel and, get this, write speeches for the governor of Georgia. All the while, I was trying to get a job—any job—in broadcasting somewhere in Atlanta.

It would've been nice then to have known that my Talkmaster days were ahead.

Oh! Speaking of the night auditor job at the hotel! This particular motel was a popular stop for state legislators when they found the need for a quick one-hour evening nap during sessions of the General Assembly. I often wondered when they checked in for their briefest of stays with local ladies of the night if they thought to themselves, "Gee, that clerk looked oddly like that skinny kid who's writing speeches for the governor."

Probably not. We're talking the Georgia General Assembly here—not the brightest string of lights on the tree.

So how on earth would a night auditor wind up putting words

---

[4] I do need to report here that after I found a job and an apartment, I went back to College Station to pick up the Cajun and bring her to Atlanta. We tried for four more years to make this thing work... it didn't. But it did set the wheels in motion that led me to Donna. Everything happens for a reason.

into the mouth of our much-maligned governor?

Yes, as my detractors will readily tell you, the governor for whom I wrote speeches was Lester Maddox. I was between jobs and looking for something more challenging than monitoring orders for carpet. Imagine that.

Maddox periodically held what he called "People's Days" at his office. Anyone who wanted a word with the governor could get in line. When they reached the front, they would have a minute or two to say their piece. No metal detectors, in those days. The vast majority of people in those lines were there asking for some sort of government assistance or pleading for the release of their (completely innocent) husband or son who was resting in a Georgia prison.

So, there I was in that line. I was going to get a job in the governor's office. I had taken a civil-service exam about two years earlier, but turned down the offer to be a prison guard. It seemed that every single person who took the civil service test at that time was automatically offered a job as a prison guard. Having somewhat higher aspirations, I demurred. I wanted to be on TV or radio, and decided working for the governor was going to be a step in that direction.

When Maddox asked what he could do for me, I responded that it was more like what I could do for him. I told him that his speeches were basically boring, and that I was the guy to put a little life in them.

Yup. I did.

He looked at me and asked, "See that guy over there? That's my executive secretary. Go over there and tell him that you're starting tomorrow as my speechwriter."

Well, that "guy over there" turned out to be Zell Miller, who later served as a Democrat Senator from Georgia—and is perhaps best known for his speech seconding the nomination of George W. Bush for his second term as President.

Working for the governor was interesting, to say the least. Most of the speeches I wrote concerned economic development plans in the various areas of Georgia where Governor Maddox would visit.

I bring this up, because now—over 40 years later—the name Lester Maddox is generally associated with segregation, racism and axe handles. (They were really pick handles, by the way.) What is not generally known is that Lester Maddox created more high-level positions in state government for black Georgians than any previous governor. He appointed the first black Georgia state trooper.

Years later, MLK-confidant and renowned civil rights leader Hosea Williams would say that Lester Maddox did more for black people in Georgia than any governor before or since. Most stories have two sides. I just wanted to touch on his other.

No apologies.

Oh, and that short-lived night auditing career? It nearly ended my story before it really got started. I had signed on to audit the daily books at one particular downtown motel, and scored a better day job on the very day I was to report to work. So I didn't show up.

The very next night, the man who ended up with the auditing job was shot and killed in a late-night robbery.

I guess I was meant to stick around to aggravate—I mean *entertain*—the masses.

OK... LET'S GET TO THE RADIO THING HERE

Throughout my early-job history in Atlanta, I had one over-arching goal: I wanted to get into broadcasting in some capacity. I didn't care what it was. News cameraman for a TV station? Fine. Reporter? Super. After all, that degree I had barely missed was in Journalism. It was combined, by the way, with Aerospace Engineering—I also wanted to be a science writer. But, most of all, I wanted to be a talk show host.

During my years at Rich's, I would venture out to interview with radio and TV stations throughout the Atlanta area. Everyone was perfectly nice, but the response was generally, "Hey kid, you left College Station, Texas, and now here you are in a major media market like Atlanta, trying to get a job in radio or TV. Go somewhere smaller and pay your dues, then call us back."

Well, sorry, that just wasn't going to work for me. "No" wasn't an acceptable answer—in fact, I've already told you how "no" typically inspired me—so I just kept plugging away. Something, some-where was going to break.

I was right. *I just didn't know it was going to be someone's heart.*

Around that particular time, a new talk station was making its debut in Atlanta: WRNG – Ring Radio. WRNG was a 1,000-watt, daytime-only candle in a brisk wind, but I was glued to the station almost from the moment it signed on. The morning host was an absolute hell raiser named Herb Elfman.

Elfman had a rather interesting history. He started out calling Bob Grant's radio show in Los Angeles. His calls, as I understand it, became so frequent—and Elfman became such a pest—that he was eventually banned from calling the show. I don't know how Elfman managed to get from California to Georgia, but there he was on Ring Radio with his own show.

I decided that, if being a caller was a way to get a foot in the door of talk radio, a caller is what I would be. I started calling Elfman's show every time I could. I would make sure that I had something interesting to say. And I would get right to it as soon as I heard the click on the line—none of this "How are you doing?" or "I really love your show" stuff. I tried to grab his attention in the first six words—and usually succeeded.

Over the months, Elfman and I became friends. I would hear that he was speaking somewhere, and made it a point to show up and introduce myself. Soon, he invited me to the station to watch him do the show. I used that opportunity to pester management for a job. No luck. Always the same line: "Go get some experience in a smaller market and get back to us."

Screw that. I liked Atlanta—and I was determined to break into radio there, one way or another.

Well, then it happened. A tragic scenario—but it happened, nonetheless.

When Herb came to Georgia, he, too, had been suffering from an episode of domestic intranquility back in California. After es-tablishing himself in Atlanta, he decided it was worth a shot to return to California to see if he could patch things up with his wife.

As I understand it, the discussion went something like this: Herb asked his wife if she would reunite with him and move to Atlanta. She said no. Herb pulled out a gun and shot himself.

Shot himself dead.

It was late on a Sunday night. I was watching the 11 o'clock newscast when I heard the news: Ring Radio talk show host Herb Elfman was dead in California of a self-inflicted gunshot wound. I was horrified. I had genuinely liked him and his loss was tragic.

Stunned, my mind also began to race about the possibilities. (Just who do you think gave Rham Emmanuel that "Never let a good crisis go to waste" idea? Me, of course.) So I set the alarm for 4 a.m. and went to sleep. I usually don't mess with alarm clocks—but here was an opportunity I wasn't going to miss.

Ring Radio, as I said, was a daytime-only AM radio station. At 5 each morning, they signed on a low power. Herb's show had started at 6. So, there I was, sitting outside the front door of the radio station in a lawn chair, reading a newspaper and drinking coffee when the station manager showed up.

He had an engineer and the afternoon talk show host in tow. The manager, Ray Stansfield, was familiar with me, thanks to my constant harassment asking for a job. The conversation went something like this:

"What are you doing here?"

"Haven't you heard? Herb isn't going to make it. He's dead."

"I know, you insensitive prick, but why are YOU here?"

"To take his job, of course!"

"I've told you… NO. You don't have the experience. Bob here is going to do Herb's show."

"Well, who's going to do *his* show?"

"Someone on the staff will fill in for him. He's only on 90 minutes and, in three weeks, we're going to be signing off earlier (due to earlier sunsets), so his show will be gone."

"OK, fine. Let me do his show for three weeks."

Well, that must have sounded like a pretty good idea to him, because Stansfield said yes. (*He said yes!*) He told me to show up that afternoon and be ready to impress. I was.

I took those 90 minutes a day and ran like hell with them. Two weeks later, they took Bob off of Herb's show and put him back to do the remaining week of the 90-minute show—*and put me in Herb's place!*

That was it. Forty-two years later, I'm still doing talk radio in Atlanta—and now it's nationwide.

MEMORIES OF *WRNG-* RING RADIO

There were some good memories from those early days at *WRNG.*

I hadn't developed the well-honed propensity for explosive rants for which I am now known and honored. We had to literally beg for callers, at times. In desperation, we would put a psychic on the air, or an astrologer.

Somebody just shoot me.

Those guests would do nothing but produce a string of callers who would say, "I was born on March 13th—tell me about myself" or "Can you tell me if I'm going to find true love?" How that station stayed on the air, I'll never understand.

My initial salary for the show, by the way, was $9,000 a year.

To supplement my income, the show allowed me to do an auction show on the weekends. Here's how that worked: During the week, I would go to various merchants around Atlanta and ask them for some merchandise—from blenders to lawn mowers to color TV sets. I would then auction those items off on the air, while giving a mini-commercial for the merchant.

"Next we're going to auction off this beautiful 19-inch color TV from Bob's Appliances at 2540 Peachtree Street, where they sell and service all major brands of televisions."

The radio station kept half the money and I got the other half. I essentially doubled my income, not to mention my workload, with this show.

Remember Hugh Hefner's girlfriend Barbie Benton? Yup! Cute as she could be. I had her on the show once. Well… OK. I *interviewed* her on the show once. She couldn't pronounce the word "pornography"—called it "phonography." That was OK, though. I was all eyes. She was one of the prettiest ladies I ever interviewed.

Phonography and all.

Then, there was Sylvia Krystel. She starred in the soft-porn movie *Emmanuelle* in 1974. Don't, whatever you do, look up a current picture of her if you remember what she looked like in that movie.

Well, I had her on the show, and she was a perfect stunner. I was impressed that she actually owned a string of gas stations. They were in Germany, I think. Somehow, that didn't fit with the Emmanuelle in the movie.

Being the all-American male, I was thoroughly tongue tied during the entire interview. She knew it and played it for all she was worth. I was in a fountain-pen stage then, and was holding one in my hand, when I gestured while asking a question. There it was—a streak of ink across her chest and running down her cleavage. She looked at me, handed me a tissue, and told me to clean it off.

I didn't sleep for three days.

Lawrence Welk was also a great guest. Asked me if I could sing. I tried a few lines from Oklahoma—he told me to forget it.

Arthur Godfrey was another memorable guest. Sean Hannity wouldn't have a clue who Arthur Godfrey is. For years after that interview, I received a case of grapefruits every Christmas from him.

Mind you, I would have preferred to receive some melons from Sylvia.

Every time a guest showed up for any of the hosts, we had them sign the inside of the door to the studio with a huge marker. Over the years, the autographs really became impressive—all the way from Barry Goldwater to Jimmy Carter. There was Lassie's paw print, Hank Aaron, actors, movie stars—you name it.

One night, the clean-up crew—most of whom couldn't speak English—thought they would do us a favor and paint that door with all the scribbling on it. *True story.* What a treasure that door would be today.

By the way, our news director at *WRNG* was a wonderful man named Bruce. I'm not going to mention his last name, because I haven't been able to contact him for permission. Considering the fact that he was a World War II vet, chances are he might not even be around, anymore.

That WWII vet thing? Well, there's another story.

When victory was declared in Europe, Bruce joined in the celebrations with the rest of the troops. That's how he came to be standing on the roof of a train to get a good view as some American troops marched by. Bruce raised his arms over his head in celebration—and they touched the overhead wire feeding electric power to the train. The resulting shock literally burned Bruce's legs off. By the time he came to work at *WRNG*, he was sporting two wooden legs.

One fine day, the studios of *WRNG* suddenly came alive with a swarm of insects—termites, in fact. Being the caring people that we were, we rushed into the newsroom, grabbed Bruce, and carried him outside. I'm certain we saved his legs from termite damage.

DEADLY DELAY SYSTEMS

You probably already know that most talk radio stations have systems that delay what's allowed onto the air. These systems take the programming—the host and caller—and run their conversation through a mechanism that captures about seven seconds for screening and then sends it to the transmitter for broadcast.

Most people assume that delay systems exist to ensure some rogue caller doesn't succeed in being profane on the air—and, yes, they serve that purpose very well. What you don't know is that, on my show, this oh-so-useful system has been engaged far more often to censor me, not the callers. You might have noticed I can get a little *insensitiiiiiive* when I speak.

Oh, the stories I could tell! One of my favorites is of a delay system gone terribly awry—but it includes a rather profane reference. Be prepared. First, let me try to explain how this system worked in the old days—yes, *my* days—so you can understand how this awful error came to happen:

At *WRNG*, the delay process consisted of tape cartridges simi-lar to those old 8-track cassette tapes some of you used to play in your car back in the dinosaur days. Remember those? But, rather than 40 minutes of tape playing about 10 music selections, these cartridges had just 10 or so seconds of tape on them.

To accomplish its task, the cartridge machine was modified in a pretty simple way: You just switched things around, so that the tape would first run through the playback head, then an erase head, and *then* a recording head. When the tape passed over the recording head, the programming would be captured.

That recorded moment took 10 seconds to cycle through the loop and reach the playback head and get sent to the transmitter. Then the erase head would clean things off to get ready for the record head to begin again.

Got the picture?

If someone called to suggest that the host perform... oh, let's just say a physical impossibility... the board operator would sim-ply disconnect the caller and hit the eject button on the tape car-tridge. With the offending language out of the way, the cartridge would be set aside to have new tape installed.

Seeing the first signs of a weak link, yet?

After the same piece of tape has been run over three magnetic heads every 10 seconds for a few hours, it begins to wear a bit thin. So, the Georgia-Tech engineers (haha, not really—they were really Longhorns) developed a system to rotate delay tapes. As one was ejected, it would be added to a stack of others waiting to be re-loaded with fresh tape. The engineer would then grab a tape from a stack of newly reloaded ones, put it in the cartridge machine, press the little green button—and it was off to the races.

Fast forward to the day of infamy.

I forget who was on the air—wasn't me—but some caller de-cided to try to get an obscenity past the censor system. As soon as the caller heard the BEEP indicating he was on the air, he said, **"Good morning! I just have one thing I want to say: *F*____**

YOU!" (Give me credit, at least, for not spelling it out. Or maybe this is my prudish editor censoring me, again.)

The engineer did his job, admirably: Punch the button, remove the ejected tape, insert fresh tape, back in business… *voila.*

There was just one problem: The engineer did MOST of his job well—right up to the point where he was *supposed* to put the ejected tape into the reload pile.

Now you see the problem.

That cartridge, with the caller's best wishes, was sitting there like a time bomb in a stack of what was meant to be harmless, reloaded fresh tape. All it needed was to be queued up for action.

Fast forward to the tape's *second* appearance on *WRNG.*

It just *had* to be on a Sunday morning—and just *had* to be during a call-in show hosted by a local Baptist preacher. Fate would not allow this to happen any other way.

So here, dear readers, is how the whole event played out on the air. I don't recall the name of the show, the church or the preacher, but this is what *WRNG's* listeners heard:

"It's 8 o'clock and welcome to the Calvary Baptist Hour! Here, to share the message of Christ, is Calvary Baptist Church Pastor Mike Anderson!" [At this very moment, the engineer switches tape carts]
"Good morning! I just have one thing I want to say! F____ YOU!"

At that point, the delay kicked in and the show continued with the good pastor, who was oblivious to what had just happened, delivering a short Bible lesson. His message was followed by an invitation for listeners to call in.

Call in they did!

Since the pastor and the engineer had both been listening to live programming on their headphones, they had no idea what was about to erupt. The only ones who had heard Pastor Anderson's rather unique homily were the listeners at home—most of his parish, to be exact—and you can rest assured they jammed the phone lines to express displeasure with their man of God.

It didn't take many phone calls before Pastor Anderson gathered his belongings and stormed out of the station, heading back to do damage control at his church.

Talk about fire and brimstone!

Today, delay systems are handled digitally—by a computer. They're seldom used these days. I guess callers know their obscenities aren't going to get through, so they don't even try, anymore.

Sometimes, I miss the good ol' days.

SCREWING WITH THE ON-AIR GUY

From Day One in my radio career, it has always been great sport to try to screw with the person on the air. Remember the tarantula story? More often, however, the object was to get them to lose their concentration and either laugh or mess up their script. I'm thinking it's a good thing that airline pilots don't do this kind of stuff—like lighting someone's approach chart on fire.

Did I say "on fire?" Yup. Seems I did.

Back in the "olden days," we had teletype machines in almost every radio station news room. That was the *clickety clickety* noise you would hear in the background. When the announcer got in front of the microphone for a newscast, he would more often than not have a stack of this teletype paper in front of him.

Just as he started the newscast, some jerk—often me—would reach around and light his news copy on fire. That's right—on FIRE. Real flames. You haven't lived until you've seen a radio newsman trying to read flaming news copy and racing to get to the end of the story before it is burnt to a crisp.

There were other ways to screw with the on-air guy. One very common way was simply to "drop trou" and press your huge pasty-white arse right into the window in front of the poor sap on the mic. Most radio professionals aren't the least bit phased by this plebeian effort—and no, I never tried that one.

A more effective and unique way to disrupt a newscast would involve—or seem to involve—some basic bodily functions.

Let me paint a picture: Before the newscast, you head into the studio to place a trashcan in the corner. Make sure the trashcan is visible to the announcer. Then, in the middle of the newscast, you walk quietly into the news booth and up to the trashcan—carefully hiding a glass of water. You face the trashcan in the corner, loudly unzip your pants—and then start pouring the water into the trash-can. There is no way the poor announcer is not going to believe that he has a moron in the studio taking a whiz into the trashcan during his newscast.

And then there's the announcer, the newsman, the sportscaster who absolutely cannot be broken. The consummate professional that wouldn't break stride if he suddenly discovered that his news copy was printed on the belly of a live rattlesnake.

Such a man was Atlanta sports legend Hank Morgan. I'm not up to speed on Hank's entire history in Atlanta, but I do know that he went far enough back to have been the play-by-play announcer for The Atlanta Crackers. I also knew that absolutely NOTHING could break his concentration while on the air. The entire studio would burn down around him and he wouldn't miss a beat... but *ohhhh* how people tried.

And so it came to pass on one memorable day... Hank Morgan finally lost it. Here's how it happened— and, yes, names will be withheld to protect the demented:

One particular *WRNG* employee (not me, I swear) was just determined to get to Hank. As soon as the newscast started, this person opened the door and walked into the news booth—butt naked. He crawled up on the table—Hank never missed a beat. He straddled Hank's news copy—Hank read on. He squatted over Hank's news copy, acting like he was going to drop a deuce right then and there—Hank moved on to the sports.

Our prankster, now disappointed and giving up, started to slowly climb down from the table. Just as his rear end passed in front of Hank's news copy, he cut one. Not one of those that sounded like tearing canvas. Not even like tearing paper. It was the dreaded SBD: Silent, But Deadly.

Though it made nary a sound, there was a disturbance in the air currents across the desk that caused Hank's stack of news copy to flutter, shall we say, in the breeze. That was it. Hank was done. He literally fell out of the chair onto the floor laughing.

Cut to commercial.

AND THEN THEY FIRE ME — AGAIN

You're nobody until somebody fires you.

For me, it happened about three-and-a-half years into my tenure at *WRNG*. Let's face it. Talk radio was a new genre at the time, and there wasn't exactly a huge supply of talented professionals ready to manage and program talk radio stations. The progression of program directors at *WRNG* finally led to a man named Harry Davey.

Harry, a former district director for The John Birch Society and one of the hosts on *WRNG*, was a good friend but, frankly, he didn't have a clue how to go about programming a talk station. So, he did what anyone would do: He called other, more established program directors to ask for advice, and they were only too willing to share their experiences.

One particular program director made a suggestion that changed my course and career. He told Harry, like it was gospel, that no talk show host was good for more than three years in any market.

Uh oh. I had been there for over three years.

The call came: Would I please visit Harry in his office?

The axe fell.

The pink slip flew.

The eagle dumped on my head.

I was fired.

Oh, they were very nice about it. They gave me a six-week notice, allowed me to produce some demo tapes, and said that I could have the use of a company car to drive around the East Coast to see if I could get another gig—but my days on Ring Radio were at an end. Some newcomer named Ronn Owens would be in the next day to take over my show.

Yeah… *that* Ronn Owens.

I got busy immediately and produced a demo tape of some of my best moments on the air. The Barbi Benton "phonography" interview was there, as were some interesting outtakes of me berating local bigots.

I mailed those tapes to about a dozen radio stations up the East Coast, and relaxed a day or two to give those tapes time to arrive on program directors' desks. Then Donna and I hit the road, certain there would be multiple job offers. How were we going to decide which one to accept?

The road trip began: Charlotte, Raleigh, Norfolk, Philadelphia, Baltimore, Newark, New York City. In most cities, the program directors were just too busy to see me.

"Sorry, he won't have time to talk to you today. He'll contact you if he decides he wants to talk to you."

I did manage to talk to one program director in Baltimore. Nothing to offer, but at least he was cordial. New York City? Are you kidding me? This kid from Atlanta is up here in the media capital of the world trying to get a talk show gig?

They wouldn't even allow me to park my car.

And so it was on to Schenectady, New York—hope to General

Electric and their flagship radio station, 50,000 watt barn-burner *WGY*, one of America's (at the time) premiere talk radio stations.

Donna and I checked into the Holiday Inn. I had already called ahead and the program director had listened to my tape and agreed to talk with me. I left Donna in the room and headed to the *WGY* studios.

Lightning struck!

After talking for about an hour, the program director (wish I could remember his name) offered me a job—a talk gig on a 50-kilowatt talker! I would be doing the early evening show from about 7 to 10 and would be heard across the entire Northeast.

Paydirt! They were going to start me at $15,000 a year! Could this get any better?

I flew ecstatically back to the Holiday Inn. This was around 1973 and there were no cell phones then. I raced to the room, eager to share the news of our tremendous good fortune.

When I walked into the room, Donna was standing at the window, looking out at a perfectly dreadful, cold and rainy September day in Schenectady. She heard me come in and turned around—and I saw the tears in her eyes.

"What's the matter, sweetheart?"

"I hate this place! It's ugly and depressing!"

I paused a moment. Should I share the good news?

"So do I," I said. "Tell you what. I'm going to go downstairs and check out, and we're heading right back to New York City. We'll see the sights for a few days, and head back home to Atlanta."

She smiled and I was out the door. Downstairs, I found a pay phone and called the *WGY* program director. I told him (yes, lied) that a job offer had come through back home in Atlanta and that I wouldn't be able to accept his offer after all.

I checked out, we loaded the car, and hit the road south.

As soon as I got back to Atlanta, I found a job—well, a series of jobs—and applied for law school. See what I mean about seemingly unimportant events changing the entire course of your life?

Where would I be today if Donna had not been crying when I

opened that door?

Within a few weeks, I enrolled in the John Marshall Law School in Atlanta. To pay my way, I sold life insurance, worked for the United States Postal Service side by side with my wife, and studied during my off time.

After a few months, the phone call came: Ronn Owens, it seemed, was leaving Ring Radio to go to San Francisco and work at KGO. (So far as I know, he is there to this day.) The listener reaction to my having been fired had been less than positive—and Harry Davey had stopped listening to idiot program directors from other markets.

After having been gone about six months, I was offered my old job back—at double the salary.

I said yes. *I'm not an idiot.*

Oh and about that job offer at *WGY* in Schenectady: Almost 30 years passed before I finally told Donna that I had come bursting into that Holiday Inn with a job offer.

If I had it all to do over again, I would make the same choice today. She is, after all, the Queen.

TRACKING TWO CAREERS

To facilitate my law studies, we moved my show to the afternoons on *WRNG*. I attended law school until around 1, then off to the studio. I wasn't a particularly dynamic host during those three years. Most of my time was taken up with my law studies, but I managed to hold down some pretty fair ratings while building a loyal Atlanta listenership.

I took the Georgia Bar Exam in February of 1977. I remember that, in the months leading up to the exam, my mother constantly reminded me not to be disappointed when I failed the first time around.

Nice negative programming, huh?

Hate to say it, but I had to temporarily cut my parents off during those final two months. Negativity wasn't allowed. I decided that I would call them *after* the test. I was so determined to eliminate any possible distractions while I studied that I went to sleep early each evening, and then got up around 2:30 to study four hours before heading to school.

I wanted to be a lawyer[5] and here, I believe, is an important lesson in positive thinking: If you want something, live your life as if you already have it. So, when the Bar exam came along, I dressed up in a three-piece, pin-striped suit for the test. I wanted to look the part.

The State of Georgia allowed third-year law students to take the Bar exam before their graduation. So, even after the exam, there was more studying and finals.

About one week before graduation, we were still waiting for the Bar exam results to come out. I remember that I was on the air when a call came through from DeKalb County Superior Court Judge Curtis Tillman.

"Congratulations, lawyer!" he said.

"Huh?"

"Yeah! You passed the bar exam!"

At that moment, someone at the station came into the studio with a bottle of champagne. I was completely wasted in about 10 minutes. How I wish I had a tape of that show today. It was the only time I've ever been completely plowed on the air—well, except for that time someone delivered some brownies to Ring Radio. But that's another story.

About three years after I started my law practice, I began experiencing problems with *WRNG*. They could not accept that my primary focus was on practicing law. The radio show would always come in second when hard decisions, such as court appearances, had to be made. So we parted company. That, I thought, was the end of my radio career—and then *WGST* came along.

---

[5]Actually, I had thought about being a lawyer since high school. My very first girl-friend, Sharon, gave me a law book for my 17th birthday. She left me for some pasty-faced kid, because he could speak French. When we broke up, I broke out. Gawd, what a zit farm.

THE WGST YEARS — AND PRACTICING LAW

My years with *WGST* began with occasional guest hosting. The response from listeners to my time on the air was so great that we immediately started talking about a full-time gig. I explained to them that, though I would be willing to do a morning show, the law practice would take precedence whenever there was a scheduling conflict. They agreed.

The pay could only be described as, well, *dismal*. But I loved doing talk radio and, with my income from the law practice, I didn't mind.

To be candid, I found practicing law to be a perfectly miserable way to earn a living. The truest thing anyone told me as I hung out the old shingle was that, as a lawyer, my worst enemy would turn out to be my client. I had no idea how true this was.

I began my practice renting office space from an attorney named Bill Carlisle in Decatur, Georgia. Bill's grandfather had been a Georgia Supreme Court Justice, and his father had just been elected to the State Court bench—hence the empty office.

Bill was absolutely one of the most brilliant men I have ever met. When a question of law would come up, he would think for a second, then tell me to go look at "*So and So vs. Everwho at 23 Ga. 243*" for my answer. I think this guy had memorized every State Supreme Court and Court of Appeals case in Georgia history and quite a few federal cases as well.

I will never forget that horrible day in November of 1980 when tragedy again fell. Donna was working for me at the time, and a call came from Nassau in the Bahamas.

Bill, his wife Sandee, and another couple were vacationing in the Bahamas and had been ambushed by a shotgun-wielding man as they were driving away from a beach. As Bill tried to pass the ambush, the man opened fire.

Bill was the most seriously wounded, but he managed to drive the others to safety before he slumped over the steering wheel of the rented Jeep. He died later that afternoon in a Nassau hospital.

Donna had to break the news to Bill's parents. Nassau authorities later arrested and convicted a few locals for the crime, and sentenced them to life in prison. To this day, I'm not convinced these were the guilty men. I've always suspected that Bahamian authorities were anxious to put someone away for this crime, in order to diffuse a major story that might hurt the tourism business. People simply won't visit Nassau if they worry they're going to be blown away while driving around the island.

From that point on, I was on my own—a solo practice.

One thing I did love was trials. You can just imagine how much I enjoyed cross examining someone or performing in front of a jury. It was the trial preparation I hated.

One of my first trials was a criminal case—the one and only criminal trial I ever handled. I represented a drunk driver—not just any drunk driver, but a nationally known drunk driver. He had been a guest on my show and, when he was later arrested for DUI, he called me. After all, whom else did he know? He insisted on pleading "not guilty" and demanded that we try the case. So we did.

The jury's verdict? Not guilty.

My client knew he had been drunk. I knew he had been drunk. The judge knew he had been drunk. The cop knew he had been drunk. But I somehow managed to convince the jury otherwise.

I was so horrified that I had actually managed to get a drunk driver exonerated that I pledged then and there never to take another drunk driver to trial—and I never did.

The Role of the Defense Lawyer

Yes, I just told you that I got an obviously guilty client exonerated. Now let me share what I think—and what you should think, if I do say so myself—about criminal defense lawyers. I probably should bury this as a footnote, but then you wouldn't read it.

Government, whether federal or local, has one unique power that none of us has: Government, and only government, can deprive you of your right to life, liberty or property through the use of deadly force.[6]

Our founding fathers knew it was necessary that government have these extraordinary and exclusive powers, so they devised a system to keep those powers in check: the right to a trial by a jury of your peers. In order to deprive you of your property (fine you), your liberty (confine you) or your life (execute you), the government must first gather together some of your fellow citizens and convince those people of your guilt beyond a reasonable doubt.

If the government fails to carry that burden of proof, you walk.

The role of the defense attorney is *not* to get his client off.[7] His role, instead, is to hold the government—the government that has the exclusive right to use deadly force—to its Constitutional responsibility to prove guilt beyond that reasonable doubt. I want

[6]Actually, you do have the right to use deadly force in only one instance—and that is in defense of your or another person's life. In some states, you'll get your butt in a crack for doing even that!

[7]I really hate that phrase, but how else are you going to say it?

you to imagine the abuses the government would eagerly heap upon the people if defense attorneys were not there to stand between you and them.

The criminal defense attorney is very much like that cop—the one you dislike, because he wrote you a speeding ticket you didn't deserve—who later ends up standing between you and a thug with a gun. As the country song says, *"How Do You Like Me Now?"*

Take a moment and let that work its way into your brain.

Meanwhile, let me answer a question that lots of my listeners seem to like to ask: Do I have any interesting stories to share about my law practice? *Oh hell yes!* Trouble is, those stories all involve clients. Even though I'm not currently practicing (I'm on an inactive status with the Georgia Bar), there's still that lawyer-client confidentiality thing.

I did have one famous client. That would be Olympic bronze medalist (he was robbed... should have had the Gold), three-time heavyweight champ Evander Holyfield. I was his lawyer from shortly after the 1984 Olympics until the December after he defeated Buster Douglas for his first heavyweight title. Needless to say, those were some interesting years.

One anecdote about Evander? Never, in all those years, did I ever hear one single swear word from that man. His mother would have beaten his tail.

OK. Just *one* Holyfield story:

In late 1987, the Holyfield team flew to St. Tropez—that's in France—for a fight against Ossie Ocasio. Some of you more worldly types might immediately associate St. Tropez and the French Riviera with somewhat scantily clad women—meaning topless—on the beaches. We were actually staying across the bay in St. Maxim for that fight, right on the beach—a beach full of young ladies (and old) who could only afford bikini bottoms.

Now you may have heard this from other people who have visited these beaches, but I'm here to tell you that what they say is true. When you first walk onto one of these beaches, you are, of course, completely captivated by all of the funbags bouncing around. This, believe it or not, lasts for about 20 minutes. After that, amazingly enough, you'll find yourself drawn to the ladies wearing swimsuits with actual tops.

Go figger.

So there we were, Evander and I, sitting at a table next to the boardwalk, eating spaghetti. Some heavily endowed—and top-less—woman walking down the boardwalk recognized Evander and decided she was going to sit down and have a chat. She walked up to our table, pulled out a chair and, uninvited, sat down.

Now did I mention that she was *endowed*? Yup! So much so that her accoutrements were actually hanging there below the table as she sat. Apparently they were quite heavy as well. This lady proceeded to reach down with both hands, pick those puppies up, lean forward and drop them on the table. They fell with such a resounding thud that the table shook and our plates and glasses all jumped at least an inch into the air.

That was it: Evander completely lost it. I thought he was going to need oxygen.

Me? Have you ever seen someone's eyes bugged out like a stomped-on bullfrog?

I can picture that scene so clearly that I'm still traumatized.

By the way, The Champ went on to beat Ocasio in the 11th round.

Being an attorney sometimes meant enduring a grueling pace. Toward the end of my active practice of law, I was working in the stunningly exciting area of commercial real estate closings. In particular, I was helping a lender out of New England close renovation and acquisition loans for hotels and motels.

There just aren't enough words to tell you how exciting that was!

On more than one occasion, I made a 24-hour round trip to Phoenix or Los Angeles to close a loan. Once, I flew from Atlanta to St. Louis, closed a loan, then flew to Los Angeles, closed another loan, and flew back home to Atlanta. All in one day—back home and in bed by midnight.

That is inhumane.

This went on for a few years, and the money was actually pretty good. Not only that but, as a closing attorney, you wrote yourself the checks for your fees from the loan proceeds. No billing. No collecting.

The hours were the problem, though. I was often in the law office at 5:30 in the morning and worked until 8. Then I headed for the WGST studios and did my talk show from 9 to noon. Some fast food on the road and I was back in the office by 1.

Several nights a week, I would get a call from Donna around 10 telling me to close up and get home.

My contract with *WGST* was set to expire in September of 1992, and something had to give. I just could not keep this schedule any longer—not if I wanted to keep my family. I was either going to devote my full work efforts to practicing law, or to radio, but not to both. So Donna and I talked.

"Where could you make the most money?"

"Oh, practicing law, I'm sure."

"What do you like doing?"

"The radio show."

"Then do the radio show. Things will work out."

This is more evidence that I picked the right Queen.

I gathered together tax returns from the past three years and presented them to the management at *WGST*.

"This," I said, "is what I've been making practicing law and doing my radio show for the past three years. When my contract is up, I'm going to quit one job or the other. If you can match my total income here with a new contract, I'll sign up."

I am, to this day, completely unable to explain what happened next.

I was working for *WGST* for a combination of cash and commercial minutes. I owned a block of commercial minutes on my show every day that I could sell to advertisers. Oh… and yes. I did declare the income from selling those commercial minutes on my tax returns. Remember, I was a practicing attorney and didn't want a brush with the tax Gestapo.

When *WGST* made an offer for a new contract, they took away the commercial minutes and replaced them with a very small increase in salary. The salary increase would have made up for about one-fourth of the income I was earning selling those commercials.

In other words, *WGST* and its parent company Jacor offered me a literal <u>cut</u> in pay to work for three more years!

I handed the offer back to the *WGST* general manager and told him that the offer was so absurd I wasn't even going to counter it. If they wished to put a better and more realistic offer on the table before my contract expired, I would give it my full consideration.

In the meantime, I started making plans to expand my law practice to full time.

It was around that time that a man named Marc Morgan contacted me. He was moving to Atlanta from Chicago to take the reins of the Cox Enterprises radio cluster in Atlanta. Atlanta-based Cox Enterprises owned the *Atlanta Journal and Constitution, WSB-TV, Channel 2,* and *WSB AM and FM.*

Morgan wanted to have breakfast.

So, early one morning, before my *WGST* show, he and I met at the Original Pancake House on Peachtree Street for some pancakes. After a few minutes, he told me he wanted me to come to work at *WSB.* I liked Marc immediately, but told him that I was under contract at *WGST.*

I explained that, if they didn't meet my demands for an increase in pay, I would, in all likelihood, begin to practice law full time. I thanked him for his vote of confidence, and left.

As the end of my contract approached, I heard absolutely NOTHING from *WGST* management. By the last day of my contract, I had completely cleaned out my office and removed all of my belongings from the station. I signed off the show at noon— and walked out of the station without ever hearing another word.

That afternoon, I got a call from an agent I had hired to explore talk radio opportunities. Would I be willing to meet with him the next morning for breakfast? Sure—it wasn't like I had a radio show to do.

So Saul Foos and I met at the Buckhead Ritz Carlton for break-fast. He told me that we were going to go over to White Columns—the headquarters for *WSB-AM*—and talk to Marc Morgan. I agreed.

When I walked into Morgan's office, he wasted absolutely no time. He put a contract in front of me that paid me more than double what I was making practicing law *and* working at *WGST*.

Just as quickly, I accepted the offer.

As I drove back home, I was listening to a substitute host on *WGST* saying that they were filling in for *"the vacationing Neal Boortz."*

They still hadn't caught on.

It happens that, at that time, I was doing an afternoon TV show on Atlanta's *Channel 11*. The show, *BackTalk*, was scheduled to run for 12 weeks. *WGST* found out about my new gig when I an-nounced it on that afternoon's show.

My contract with *WGST* had a six-month non-compete clause. This meant that I couldn't go on the air with another radio sta-tion in the Atlanta market for six months after the expiration of my contract. I could live with that, because the contract required *WGST* to continue paying me during those six months. *WSB* was paying me at the same time.

Two paychecks, no work. *Score!*

So we hit the road towing a travel trailer. Six months traveling America—with two paychecks coming in. Not a bad gig.

Not a bad gig, that is, until we reached Boulder, Colorado.

Then the phone rang.

It was Marc Morgan calling to tell me that *WGST* had filed a lawsuit against *WSB* and me. They were claiming a right of first refusal. In other words, *WGST* was claiming that they had a right to match the contract offer made by *WSB*.

I was going to have to cut our six-month, see-America trip short and head back to Atlanta to fight their lawsuit. What a pisser.

When we got back to Atlanta a few weeks later, I decided to milk this *WGST* lawsuit for all it was worth. When the marshal showed up at my door to serve me with the lawsuit, I asked him if he would play along.

I put on a bathing suit and climbed into the hot tub on the back deck. A picture was taken of me sitting there in the bubbles, holding a glass of wine as I signed for the papers. The picture made it to the front page of *Creative Loafing*, an Atlanta weekly alternative paper.

Clearly, I was very concerned about the suit.

We'll leave out all of the legal maneuvering and machinations. *WGST* soon figured out that they were simply not going to win, so they had their attorney withdraw the suit and write a letter to the judge saying they were dismissing the action.

Stated reason? Because they had questions about my integrity.[8] Nice parting shot—try to besmirch my reputation and standing with my fellow attorneys and judges in the very county in which I practiced law. It takes a real low life as an attorney to write a letter like that without any foundation.

This was just the beginning of the war they would launch on me in the ensuing months. But no more details here on the *WGST* dirty tricks. I'm friends again with most of those people, and it would serve no purpose to go riding off into retirement leaving wounded egos and hurt feelings behind.

I will say this, though. As I write this, *WGST* is broadcasting soccer scores in Spanish. Yes, they eventually became a Spanish-language sports station.

Many years passed, however, before that happened. They engaged in a 19-year, futile effort to compete with *WSB*. Nothing worked. Their first job, of course, was to find a replacement for me. For that, they traveled to Huntsville, Alabama, and found a promising young talk show host.

---

[8]This is for you legal types out there. The restrictive covenant in the WGST contract was completely unlimited as to time and territory. WGST was claiming a right of first refusal at any time in the future anywhere in the universe. Such a contract is unenforceable as a matter of law, and WGST knew it. All they had left was to attack my integrity, tuck their tails and run.

At that point, I was cleaning up the remnants of my law practice from the law offices of a friend in the same building that housed *WGST*. I've been told the radio station's staffers would pass the word that I was in the building whenever my car was spotted in their parking garage.

On one such day, the *WGST* program director—I called him Sluggo—started wandering the building with their new talk show host. He was looking for me. When I stepped off an elevator, he walked up and said "Hey, Boortz, I want you to meet our new host. He's going to kick your ass in the ratings."

The new guy stuck out his hand.

"I'm Sean Hannity. Pleased to meet you."

To this day, Hannity remains apologetic about our first meeting. No need. I knew the "in your face" game *WGST* was playing. The irony here is that Sean and I became friends rather quickly. He had no revenge motive at all. His job was to get listeners, and that he did quite well. Obviously.

March 3, 1993 approached.

That would mark the end of my six-month exile from all radio for all time throughout the entire universe, and I would get behind the *WSB* mic.

Finally, at the age of 47, I only had one job.

NEWS TALK 750 WSB

I wonder how many times that phrase has come out of my mouth in the last 20 years. Tens of thousands, I would imagine. But right out of the gate, *WSB* made a mistake—one that we would use to our advantage later, but a mistake, nonetheless. They decided that my show would run from noon to 3 each weekday afternoon.

That was a break in my normal routine and, besides, I wasn't particularly anxious to go up against Rush Limbaugh. I wanted to compete directly with Hannity, and didn't see the wisdom in letting him get any more of a head start. But afternoons it was—and we were off to the races.

Truth be told, I didn't really break out of the starting gate all that well. I'm a morning person, usually up around 5:30. Those circadian rhythms kick in and the afternoons have been traditionally rough.

Did I listen to Hannity in the mornings? *Absolutely*! Now I listen to him in the afternoons. On one particular Friday morning—and I can't remember how long I had been on the air at *WSB* at that point—I heard Sean talking about how he and his family were going to get in a car and head out for a week's vacation as soon as the show was over.

I arrived early at *WSB* and headed straight to Marc Morgan's office, asking that he call Greg "Bugsy" Moceri, our new program director, in for a quick meeting. I told them that Hannity was leaving for vacation, and I wanted to immediately move my show to the mornings, so I could steal as many of his new listeners as possible before he got back.

Now, just as a bit of behind-the-scenes info, let me tell you: Things simply do not work this fast in radio. You don't switch shows around in the course of one day and one meeting.

I must have been particularly eloquent and forceful because, after just a few minutes, they said yes: *Do it.* We agreed that I would announce the change on my show that afternoon.

So how did I make the announcement?

Well, I waited until I was reasonably sure that Hannity and family were in the car and on the way to their vacation spot. I knew he would be listening to me, so here's what I said:

"Hey, Sean! Hannity! On your way to your vacation, are you? Well, I have a little announcement to help send you on your way. On Monday morning, we're moving my show to mornings here on *WSB*. While you're on the beach, I'm going to be hitting on your listeners. We'll see how many I will be able to capture before you get back. *Have a nice vacation!*"

Yeah, you're right. What a jerk I was!

According to Sean, he immediately called the station and told them he was coming back. That is the nature of Hannity's competitive spirit. They told him no, go on the vacation and everything would be just fine. He took their advice and continued with his family's plans.

I had a week to make my move. The war for ratings between Hannity and me was on!

All the while, our friendship was growing. During newsbreaks, we would often pick up the phone and talk to each other about most anything. Then one or the other of us would say, "News is over, gotta go!"

The relationship reached even further than Sean and me. During that time, I was writing a weekly column for *Creative Loafing,* that weekly alternative newspaper I mentioned earlier. My editor there? Jill Hannity—Sean's lovely wife, the lady that truly keeps him sane.

Ratings? Well, remember that, at the time I went on the air at *WSB,* Hannity had been building an audience for six months. I was moving to a station that just a few years prior had been running religious devotional services during the noon hour. Trust me—putting Neal Boortz on the air at *WSB* was pretty much out of character for the station and a bold move.

The upshot is that Hannity trounced me for the first two rating books—and then my mojo, not to mention my audience, started to come back. Soon after moving head to head with Sean in the mornings, *The Neal Boortz Show* was back to Number One.

This didn't bother Sean at all—he was already buying a bigger frying pan for bigger fish.

HANNITY — OJ — AND ROBERT SHAPIRO

Though we were becoming friends, the competition between Sean and me was intense. Let me tell you what that little weasel did to me one time.

This little slice of Hannity treachery happened a few months after that jury of idiots in California let OJ Simpson walk after he damned near cut the head off his ex wife.[9] OJ's defense lawyer, Robert Shapiro, wrote a book about the trial. I forgot the title—

---

[9] You do know not to give me that "innocent until proven guilty" Bolshoi, don't you? True, the government cannot punish OJ for that double murder—but that doesn't mean he didn't do it. Go back and read what I wrote about criminal defense lawyers. And by the way, let me tell you how happy I am that the butchering jerk is behind bars right now. Oh and Judge Ito? He couldn't judge a chili cook-off with one entry—and that's an officer of the court speaking. One more thing... that stunt OJ pulled with that glove? I've demonstrated that for a number of friends. I can take a glove—the same glove—and, on one try, make it look like I'm trying to force my hand through the opening of a wine bottle, and the next have that glove slide on like it is coated with butter. Why the prosecutors didn't call me as an expert glove witness I'll never understand. So there.

something like *"God, I Hope That Murdering SOB Doesn't Go Out and Kill Another Blonde Now That I've Helped Him Walk."*

I had Shapiro scheduled to go on my show at 10 one morning. Hannity, that twerp, was listening to my pre-recorded promo that morning when I announced Shapiro's appearance. He knew the PR flack that was most likely schlepping Shapiro around town, so he called her. He begged her to bring Shapiro by his show on the way to *WSB*, and promised he would get out of there in time to make my show. Naturally, it didn't work out that way.

Hannity is a charmer.[10]

At the point in his interview that he was supposed to thank Shapiro and send him on his way, Sean fluttered his eyelashes, flashed that coy little smile, and asked, "Can I talk you into staying for another segment?"

Shapiro agreed and the publisher's flack made no objection. Sooooo... when it came time for me to announce Robert Shapiro as my guest, he was nowhere to be seen. He was still in Hannity's studio.

I was, to put it simply, *PISSED.*

About 30 minutes later, I was informed that Robert Shapiro had driven up in his car at the back door. I told Royal to cover for me and I headed out back. Shapiro was still sitting in his limo, along with the publisher's flack.

Climbing in, I proceeded to read the riot act to the publisher's rep. I told her in no uncertain terms that not only was I not going to put Shapiro on, but that she did not ever need to call me again about having one of her authors on the air. I then turned on my heel, let it run for a while, and turned it off.[11] Then I stomped into the station.

No, I never did put another author on the air from that pub-

[10]It's the hair.

[11]An old Steve Allen line from "Bigger Than a Breadbox." Another great line from that book was "As the curtain rose, a nervous titter ran through the audience. Dr. Gillespie pulled out his titter pistol and shot it." Why DO I remember these things?

lisher.

As for Robert Shapiro? About three days later, I received two dozen red roses, a bottle of wine and a written apology from him. No dummy, that Robert Shapiro.

Make no mistake: I absolutely loved working for *WSB*. These were the most stand-up people for whom I had ever worked in broadcasting—and trust me when I tell you that broadcasting has its share of sleazoids. I may even get around to mentioning a few.

Still, I confess that something happened which, for the first and perhaps only time, caused me to have second thoughts about my move. That was the afternoon Hannity substituted for Rush Limbaugh on his syndicated show. *Dammit!*

If I had just stayed at *WGST*—with that ridiculous lowball offer they made—Hannity would be back judging pig calling at a county fair and I would be subbing for *The Godfather.*

It mattered not, though. Hannity already had his eyes on New York. It wasn't long until he left Atlanta with no sure thing in the Big City except a midnight gig on *WABC.* Sure seemed to work out well for him, though.

I'm genuinely happy for him.

SYNDICATION

I started becoming a bit of a pain when it came to syndication. Rush was out there, as was Dr. (Ugh) Laura. Hannity was moving to syndication, and I also wanted my chance at the big time, so to speak.

My show was owned, however, by *WSB* (Cox Radio) and they called the shots. I think it soon became clear to them that if they didn't syndicate my show, I would probably look for greener pastures when my contract was up.

So, a syndication deal was struck.

On the day we began syndication, we had perhaps 30 radio stations. The show never reached more than 240 or so. That's not a stunning number, when you consider the 600 stations that carried Rush and the eventual 500 stations that picked up Hannity's show.

I found ways to rationalize my lower numbers. One particular favorite was "More people drive Chevys than a Mercedes Benz."

Very clever, but I was always searching for more stations.

There were some advantages to staying lower key. I believe the relative comfort of being a talk radio back bencher actually made it easier for me to express myself on the air as I really wanted. I won't name names here, but have talked to other hosts with more stations than me who said they were constantly being monitored by various leftist organizations—like the NAACP, The Council on American-Islamic Relations, those phonies out of Montgomery, Alabama who call themselves The Southern Poverty Law Center, George Soros-funded Media Matters and others. These hosts seemed to feel the need to temper what they were saying on the air, out of fear of having to combat some organized protest against their show.

Well, I was never really big enough for them to bother. If they caught me, they would probably throw me back, and the truth is they weren't watching me all that closely. This enabled me to be a bit more edgy—and, I think, truthful—in expressing my thoughts and emotions on the air. It also allowed me to step right up to that proverbial edge of the cliff on many occasions without someone pushing me over.

Example? Well, let's see. How about this comment addressing the problem of illegal immigration? I suggested that the way to handle the Mexican invasion—and, yes, for a time it was truly a full-fledged invasion, especially along the Arizona border with Mexico—was to paint a huge crosswalk right down the border from Brownsville, Texas to San Diego, California. That would stop immigration in a heartbeat.

After all, who had ever seen a Mexican using a crosswalk?

Other hosts—with many more stations—would be run out of town on a burro for saying that!

Me? No uproar—and the Mexicans who did react thought it was funny as hell. They liked me, because I could say Esponge Roberto Pantalones Quadrados.

There were other obstacles in the way of true growth for my show in syndication. One was the fact that, even though I presented as a conservative talk show host, I was pro-choice.

I also never missed a chance to ridicule someone who believed that Earth was only 6,000 years old and that we, and all we see around us, actually *were* created in seven days.

In addition, I impressed upon my audience that homosexuality was a matter of genetics and not choice—another position not pleasing to the turbos.[12]

Well, as it happened, there was a major owner of talk radio stations out there who had deeply felt religious convictions. This station owner just could not see putting a conservative talk show host on their stations who wasn't going to carry the anti-choice[13] message to the listeners day after day after every freaking day. They also didn't want to face the howls of outrage that would come from turbo listeners upset over my belief in evolution.

Their stations—*their choice.*

But think about it: How many conservative talk show hosts do you know out there who are not pounding the so-called "pro-life" drum incessantly? Yeah, I thought so. Exactly *none.*

And then there was the Southern thing.

Yup, the Southern thing, because my show originated from *WSB-AM* in Atlanta, Georgia. You've heard it before, haven't you? Southern hicks. Hillbillies. Tobacco-chewing rednecks. Moonshiners. Most of us are descended from that guy who was playing the banjo on that bridge in *Deliverance*. And may the good Lord help you if we ever find you canoeing through our property on one

---

[12]"Turbos." My name for turbine-powered religious fanatics. They got spooled up every morning and ran incessantly until evening until it was time to shut down… whining all the way. We even have one in Georgia, a member of the Georgia legislature, who believes that the earth is standing still at the center of the universe and that everything you see out there is actually revolving around us!

[13]Yeah… "anti-choice" is the right phrase. If you are for a woman's right to choose, you're pro-choice. This does not mean you are in favor of abortion. It simply means that it's not your decision to make, and the person who is actually pregnant has, shall we say, skin in the game and should make the decision. The anti-abortion faction has managed to succeed in naming the two sides of this debate as "pro-life" and "pro-choice." That's asinine. It's either pro- and anti-choice or pro- and anti-life. People who believe in a woman's right to control her own reproductive functions are not "anti-life." You can mix apples with artichokes here.

of your citified weekend trips. *Soooooooeeeeeee*!

This stuff is real, folks, and we at *The Boortz Show* experienced it continuously. So did our syndicators. We had a pretty amazing record of success in syndication—ratings success, at any rate. The goal was to outperform the station—that is, to get ratings for the show that exceeded the ratings for the station as a whole.

In large part, we succeeded. In some geographical areas, we couldn't make any headway if our lives depended on it. Florida, for instance. I was golden across North Florida, from Pensacola to Jacksonville. We dominated down the East Coast as well, at least to the Melbourne area. Then across the I-4 corridor, Orlando to Tampa, and down the West Coast of Florida to Naples.

The Boortz Show did very well in those areas.

But south of Melbourne on the East Coast? *Fuhgetaboutit*! We couldn't draw flies to a dump. I was on the air for a while in Ft. Lauderdale and West Palm—"for a while" being the operative words here. Why? Because, as soon as you get south of Daytona Beach and Melbourne in Florida, you have magically arrived in New England. This is New Jersey - New York – Massachusetts – Connecticut – I-95 territory.

Venture into Southeast Florida and the "Southern" thing is in play again. Don't you dare tell these people they live in the South. They live in by-God-Boca, and don't you forget it.

Southwest Florida, on the other hand, is I-75 territory. Atlanta, St. Louis, Chicago—good stalwart Midwesterners who don't panic and run around in circles when they hear someone spout a conservative view.[14]

Anyhow, my syndicator would approach a station manager, program director or operations manager of a West Coast or Northeast talk station with all the hoopla about my show, including the rat-

---

[14] Someday, I mean to ask Rush Limbaugh why he chose to live in West Palm rather than Naples. Naples is in Collier County, Florida—the most solidly Republican county in the state—and, by the way, the county with the most golf courses per capita. Maybe I should play Chamber of Commerce here and tell you that around 2010, Collier County boasted the longest life expectancy for women in the entire country, and the second longest for men. Something in the water. Naples is sometimes referred to as Florida's Carmel. But keep this to yourself, please.

ings success stories, and they would hear, "But Neal Boortz broadcasts from Atlanta, doesn't he? That's a Southern show. Our listeners just wouldn't listen to a Southern show." Translation: "Our listeners are far too sophisticated to listen to a bunch of Southern rednecks complaining with their ignorant Southern drawls about the gummit 'comnists and Yankees.'"

Jimmy Carter didn't help things, either.

Now it can be told. Other than politicians, there may not be a group of self-proclaimed "professionals" anywhere in this country with a more severe, and often terminal, case of rectal-craniaitis than people who program talk radio stations. They wouldn't recognize a potential ratings success if it kicked them in the knee and then bit them in the ass while they were bent over in pain.

Actually, as I said earlier, this probably worked out to my advantage. The nail that sticks out the farthest gets pounded down first, and my nail really never stuck out all that far.

Hard as steel? You bet! Just short.

Well, depending upon how you measure short, that is.

Then... The Decision to Retire

My goal was to get this book finished and out there as an eBook well before my retirement. It looks like, because of my procrastination, I'm going to make it with only about 20 shows left.

Sorry, but remember, this is really for my granddaughter. She's 3 now and has no idea what a Grandpa really is, what I do for a living, and what retirement means. She thinks her Grandma lives at Cracker Barrel and, after seeing me on several TV shows, thinks that I live behind the flat-screen TV in her living room.

I signed my last three-year contract with Cox Media Group in 2009. The contract was slated to expire at the end of 2012 and Donna and I made up our minds that we were going to retire.

No, I wasn't going to retire because I was bored with what I was doing.

I can truly say that I've been one of the lucky ones who never groaned on a Monday morning about having to start another work week. In addition, I am blessed to be working with some of the most wonderful people I have ever known. You'll hear more about Belinda, Cristina, Jamie, and, of course, the late Royal Marshall a bit later.

Retire? Really? Are you serious?

Let's look at my typical news day. I'm a news and political junkie, anyway, so I certainly didn't mind spending a few hours in the evenings watching the news shows and catching up with some of my favorite and not-so-favorite columnists on the Internet. I've always been an early riser, so getting up at 5:30 to catch up on even more news and write some program notes was nothing like work for me.

The radio studio? After moving to Naples, Florida around 2004, and becoming a full-time Florida resident in 2009, all but a few of my shows have come from a studio tucked away in the fourth bedroom of our condo in Naples, overlooking the beautiful Gulf of Mexico.

It is the best equipped (thanks to our Cox engineers) and most comfortable talk radio studio I have ever seen or in which I've worked anywhere in the country. I would sit there with four computer screens in front of me, Belinda on a web cam, a big-screen TV carrying CNN or Fox News, and my own private radio-talk-show-host bathroom with a Toto.

Ask Hannity—he has done his show from that studio, as has Clark Howard.

In fact, having Hannity visit gave me great opportunity for another practical joke.

Sean asked to use my studio one day and my plan was to hire a stripper to show up at my place about an hour into his show. She would disrobe—all the way—and, just as Sean was set to start a long segment leading off his second hour, she would walk into the studio—wearing nothing—head into the bathroom, close and lock the door. Then... *nothing*.

In my great plan, the rest of us would sit out in the living room and listen to Sean to discover how he would sound to an audience who was unaware that 10 feet away from him was a beautiful, naked young woman in the bathroom—doing God knows what.

But there was a problem.

This was Naples, Florida.

No strippers.

You had to go up the road to Ft. Myers for that type of big-time entertainment, and I'll only go just so far to screw around with folks—even ones I really enjoy, like Sean.

I had it all figured out in my head. The best way for him to have handled this, if I could have pulled it off, would have been to lock the door to the studio, give the lady a towel, and have her passionately scream during every news and commercial break. I doubt that his mind would have worked the situation out that way, though.

Love him, mean it, but he is a bit of a choir boy, and I say that with the greatest love and respect.

Yeah, I like to tease Sean about his somewhat buttoned-up personality but, when the chips are down or threats appear on the horizon, there is nobody I would rather have watching my back than Sean Hannity. He's absolutely solid, and I owe him a great deal.

In any case, choosing retirement—despite so much to love and miss—has not been an easy choice. The talk show thing has never been work. It has always been a passion—but a passion with a price that I simply was no longer willing to pay. That price? It's just too restricting.

Since Day One, Donna and I have shared a passion for travel. We just love to hit the road at the drop of a hat and head somewhere new. We have a good friend, former University of Georgia Head Football Coach Ray Goff, who has pretty much the same response every time you suggest a trip to him: "I can't leave before tomorrow!"

For many years, that's the way it was with us. When I was working for WGST and practicing law, the folks at *WGST* knew that my basic rule was I would do the radio show when I could do the radio show.

My primary occupation was the law; my clients deserved no less. And, during that time, we would take a two-week vacation every three months. Why?

Because we could.

When I ran from the law in 1992 and started devoting full and serious attention to my radio career, that all came to a screeching halt. I got a limited number of vacation weeks a year, and that was it. I believe I have had three or maybe four two-week vacations in the last 20 years.

That's just not enough.

When we go on vacation, we love motorhomes. In fact, we've been taking long trips in motorhomes since 1972. Once the *WSB* gig came along, that stopped. There just weren't too many places you could go in one week.

Sometime around 2004, we decided to take two weeks and travel the West in a motorhome. We hired a couple to position that coach near a major airport out yonder so that, after my show on Friday, we could fly out and reclaim the coach. The drivers flew back to Atlanta at our expense.

Two weeks later, we met them at the Denver airport as they were stepping off their flight and gave them the keys to the motorhome out in the parking lot, and we flew back home.

As this was happening, we began to look ahead to the day when we could get in our coach with no plan, no agenda, no route, and just hit the road—for months![15]

Well, there you have it: Travel. That's the number one reason I'm walking away from a perfectly good talk show and a rather healthy income. We love to travel, Donna has had to make too many trips without me, and it's time to chase that dream.

We're set financially, thanks to Donna's sane money manage-

---

[15]That, in fact, is exactly part of the plan after retirement. We purchased the BoortzBus, a Prevost from Millennium Luxury Motor Coaches in Sanford, Florida, in early 2012, and started getting it ready to go. As you read this, we may well be on the road pulling a 4WD SUV behind, with a BMW K1200LT motorcycle sandwiched between the coach and the SUV on a lift. Kinda sucks, doesn't it?

ment skills, and we're outta here.

Want a peek at what we have planned for 2013? Hold onto your seat!

First, we'll head to Kauai, Hawaii for a few weeks immediately after the last show. When we come back, we'll hop in the Boortz-Bus for a few months. Then, in May, we'll head to the Mediterranean for a cruise from Barcelona to Venice, taking about 300 former listeners with us! Then it's back to the good ol' USA and back into the bus. This time, we'll range as far as Denali National Park in Alaska, stopping along the way at Yosemite, Yellowstone, Glacier National Park, the Oregon coast, the Canadian Rockies, Niagara Falls, across to Nova Scotia, and then we'll travel along with the changing leaves right down the East Coast into Georgia, and then finally back home to Naples.

I smile just thinking about it.

Along the way, we'll park the bus in an RV resort somewhere for a flight back to Atlanta to check in with our daughter and her husband, and try to abduct our grandchild for a week or two. After a few weeks to enjoy Thanksgiving and Christmas, I'll be off to the southern tip of Argentina to hop on a ship for a trip to Antarctica.[16]

Then, in 2014, we have trips planned on riverboats down Europe's main rivers, and perhaps a trip down the Amazon thrown in. Then we'll regroup and make some new plans. The sky—or the highway—is the limit!

Try to do that with a daily radio show.

So, *there you have it*. There is no question that I've absolutely loved this talk radio career. The decision to leave the practice of law for radio full time was one of the best of my life. Sure, I probably could have done better financially as a trial lawyer, but the tension would surely have killed me by now.

---

[16]Donna is most definitely NOT making the Antarctica trip with me. She has heard about a nasty little strip of ocean called Drake's Passage between the tip of Argentina and Antarctica. That's supposed to be the roughest ocean stretch on the planet. She wants no part of it. Looks like I'm making this trip alone.

I'll show up from time to time to fill in for other talk show hosts when they manage to beg for a week or so off. I'll also be doing daily commentaries that will be broadcast on *WSB* and any other station that would like to take a chance with them.

And, yes, the BoortzBus is equipped for broadcast, in case something happens that creates an irresistible urge in me to get on the air and raise some hell. But the travel bug—and the golf bug and the sleep-in-past-5:30 bug—now has control.

There is a lot that I will miss. I'll probably need therapy to deal with the shift from adrenaline to leisure. But, as I'm hanging out in a hammock in some exotic place, I'll console myself with fun memories of people with whom I've worked during my radio career—and some of the legions I've ticked off.

I'm not holding back, so read on.

After all, what are they going to do? Fire me?

You can't fire me! *I QUIT!*

THE BOORTZ TEAM

Many of you already know them well, but let me introduce you to my broadcast crew at *WSB*—sometimes known as "The Mothership." The mainstays in the early years were Royal Marshall and Belinda Skelton. Later, and I wish it had been sooner, Cristina Gonzalez entered the mix.

I love these people—and so do my listeners—so I'm going to let 'er rip and tell you about these amazing people.

ROYAL MARSHALL

Royal was the first member of the team at *WSB*, and the only one who was there with me at the beginning. Although Royal and Belinda were hired on the same day, Belinda was originally assigned to work with Clark Howard.

As soon as I was hired by *WSB*, Royal was told he would be

my board operator. For you non-radio types, the board operator controls the microphones, plays the bumper music to get you in and out of commercial breaks, runs the commercials, keeps an eye on all of the dials and needles and gizmos and such, updates the transmitter logs, rides herd on the delay system to protect the station's FCC license—and is just generally responsible for producing a tight product to send to the transmitters.

I guess I had somewhat of a notorious reputation, because Royal immediately started catching flack from his friends in the Atlanta broadcast community.

"Oh, that Boortz is a racist! You're going to hate working for him. He's a jerk. He's impossible to work with. What a prima donna."

And those were the nicer warnings delivered to Royal.

I suspect that some of these warnings and negative comments came from *WGST*. They were, after all, pulling no punches in their efforts to spoil my *WSB* debut.

At one point, they even made cassette tapes of comments I had made about *WSB* while on the air at *WGST* and sent those tapes to *WSB* management. Everyone found it amusing, since it was so juvenile of them. They couldn't find me saying anything all that hideous, really—just calling *WSB* "We're So Boring" and such.

A few weeks after I actually went on the air at *WSB*, the lovely folks at *WGST* sent me a wonderful rendering of me—dead—in a coffin. And there was Sean nailing the lid shut. I saved that one. No, Sean had nothing to do with it.

Anyway, Royal was certainly prepared for the worst when I started the show on March 3, 1993. I could tell he was apprehensive, so I tried hard to show him how important he would be to me and to the show, and to a successful debut on *WSB*.

I don't remember how long I had been on the air—certainly no more than a few weeks—when Royal said something to me during a commercial break about a topic I was hashing over with the callers. When I got back on the air, I said, "Royal, you just said something interesting to me during that break. Why don't you repeat it for the listeners?"

He didn't hesitate a second, and jumped right in. Over the next few weeks, I invited Royal to chime in on the air more often, and never with regrets. He was intelligent, quick and very witty.

Finally, I just told Royal—and this was on the air—"Tell you what, Royal. I enjoy your input, and so do the listeners. So, from now on, any time you have something you want to say on the air, whether you are in agreement with me or not, you have a microphone. You just hit the switch, go on the air and say your piece."

He took me up on it.

Royal was, like me, a military brat. His father had been a career soldier. This added to Royal's appeal to the listeners and to me. Military brats always seem to be a step or two ahead of the pack.

Royal had also spent some time living with his family in Germany. I'm not really sure if I ever want to learn the translations for those German phrases Royal would throw out on the air from time to time. They sure tickled him, though.

He was a huge hit with the listeners, and in no time he was widely recognized in Atlanta as more of a radio personality than he was a board operator. He had an infectious laugh and consistently cheery disposition, and oh how he loved to jump in my stuff. I've heard from many talk show hosts, both in Atlanta and across the country, who wanted to know how to cultivate their own Royal on their shows.

You can't grow them—they just occur wild in nature.

When we first started working together, he was a single guy— and apparently quite popular with the ladies. Actually, he told Donna it was easy! When he saw a lady he would like to meet, he would simply walk up and say, "Hi, I'm Royal. I'm single and I have a job."

That's not to say there weren't the occasional dramas in Royal's single lifestyle. Once, Belinda, Royal and I were in New Orleans for a promotional event for our local affiliate. The timing was a bit unfortunate, since Hurricane Katrina was bearing down on the Crescent City at the time.[17] There had been a book signing the night before, and we had a morning brunch event scheduled with listeners.

When the time came, Belinda was there. I was there. But where was Royal? The event started, food was being served—and still no Royal.

Finally, just at the point that we were really starting to get worried (New Orleans, at that time, wasn't exactly the safest city in the country), Royal showed up—groggy. Our first thought, of course, was that he had been over-served the night before.

Not so.

It seems that Royal had been at a bar in the French Quarter and started arguing with a sweet young thing about sports. Their difference of opinion must have been quite startling because, at some point, the lady head butted Royal so hard that the next thing he clearly remembered was waking up in his bed late with a hideous headache.[18]

Then there was the Viagra conversation. I have about 25 years on both Belinda and Royal, so they saw this as a reason to constantly hammer me on the air about Viagra. I guess it goes with the territory. You add on the years and automatically the assumption is that you're stocking up on the little blue pill.[19] At any rate, on one occasion, I decided to fight back:

"So, Royal. How about you? Do you use Viagra?"

"On occasion, sure!"

I was surprised at the admission.

"Really? Why? You're young, in shape—why?"

---

[17]We were, in fact, on the last flight out before the airport was closed. Too close for comfort that time.

[18]My comments about Katrina led to one of the more interesting and, to me, fun little controversies I managed to ignite on the air. Listeners became particularly upset at my suggestion that the rescue personnel should save the rich people first. After all, you'll need someone to invest in getting old businesses back on their feet and new businesses started. Are the poor going to do that?

[19]It is blue, isn't it? Seems I've heard that. Haven't ever seen one, so I couldn't tell you. Uh huh!

"Well, it's sort of like corking the bat."

Only Royal.

Belinda, of course, didn't have a clue what he was talking about, but it remained one of Royal's best lines on the show—and there were many.

He eventually took his brand of comedy and turned it into a stand-up routine that he delivered at various comedy clubs around Atlanta. I never got to attend one of his shows, but I'm told he routinely brought the house down with laughter.

For a time, Royal also had his own talk show on *WSB* in the evenings: *The Royal Treatment*. Listeners loved him.

Now here's a bit of serendipity: Shortly after Hurricane Katrina, Royal bumped into a woman he recognized in Atlanta. Her name was Annette, and they had attended high school together in St. Louis while his father was stationed there.

"Hey! I remember you!" soon turned into "I love you" and Royal and Annette were married. They had two beautiful daughters, Amira and Eva.

I'm not meaning to get overly emotional here, but it's hard to express how fond I was of Royal. Sure, we had some political differences, especially after Obama was elected, but they didn't get in the way of my feelings for him. Sometimes, during commercial or news breaks, I would be in his engineering studio talking to him and I just wanted to blurt out, "Hey man, I love you."

Never did. Wish I had.

Some of you may be a bit confused by my use of the past tense in writing about Royal.

It was January 15, 2011, about 7 in the morning, and I was all settled in with a few newspapers and a cup of coffee. The phone rang. It was Belinda—a very upset Belinda.

"We've lost Royal!" she said. She then told me that Royal had suffered a massive heart attack the night before and passed away. Words cannot describe the sorrow—the grief—the absolute shock. I was 65. He was 42. I was supposed to attend his daughters' weddings to watch him give away each bride. He was supposed to attend my funeral, not the other way around.

The week of Royal's passing had started out with some very bad weather in Atlanta. Freezing rain and ice. Royal, Belinda and Cristina were booked into a hotel within walking difference from the radio station, so that driving conditions would not keep them from getting to the studio in time. After a walk back to the hotel, Royal complained of chest pains.

Everyone just passed it off as the result of over-exertion walking in the snow and ice. It was only after Royal's death that I learned his father had died of heart failure at the age of 45, while waiting for a heart transplant.

The "what if" game is a cruel one, but we all wish to this day that we had known a little more about Royal's family history of heart disease. Those complaints of chest pains might have spurred someone into action.

RIP, Royal Marshall. You were one of a kind. God hit one out of the park when he came up with you.

He must have corked the bat.

BELINDA SKELTON

When I started my show on WSB, Belinda, though she worked there, was actually working for Clark Howard.[20] I had to go through a progression of call screeners before I lucked into Belinda.[21]

I started lobbying for Belinda to work on my show immediately after meeting her. She's one of those delightful, infectious personalities. You meet her—you love her. She's always cheerful and ready to work her fingers to the bone.

Soon after assuming the duties as my phone screener, Belinda

---

[20]Clark is currently a HLN start on TV and hosts a consumer-oriented talk show on WSB. More on him later. Stay tuned. Don't miss it.

[21]I guess I should tell it all here. One of my early screeners—back around 1993—was a stunning model/actress named Lane Carlock. The Atlanta Magazine published an article about Lane, complete with a picture and the caption "Boortz's Babe." Donna saw the picture and the caption. Interesting times. Lane is now married to Clark Howard! Geeks rule!

became the executive producer of my show. She handled all appearances, guests and the business aspects of the show. She made sure throughout my entire tenure at WSB that I never had to fill out an expense report. When we traveled, everything went on her credit card—I never had to worry about a thing.

Belinda, like Royal, had an open mic during the show. Her completely innocent comments at just the right time surely caused more than one amazed driver to leave the road and plow down about 50 yards of shrubbery.

Without question, Belinda Skelton is the most popular female radio personality in Georgia—and probably in the Southeast.

The stories about her are priceless—and, when they include her rare profanity, are even funnier.

Picture this: It's morning, before work. Belinda's in the kitchen fixing breakfast. Her youngest son, Andrew, is in a high chair. Suddenly, Andrew spots something and points to the floor:

"Look, Mommy! An ant!"

Belinda looks in the direction of Andrew's finger. Under her breath, she whispers, "That's not an ant. That's a f***ing cockroach."

At this very moment, Belinda's husband, Clark (not Howard) arrives in the kitchen. Andrew sees him and points:

"Look, daddy! A f***ing cockroach!"

Behind the island in the middle of her kitchen, Belinda is on her knees gasping for breath. She has almost passed out from laughing.

"BELINDA!" Clark knows exactly where that one came from.

"Oh, just go to work Clark. I'll handle it."

There's more.

Belinda's youngest—that's Andrew—was disqualified during his class spelling bee.

"Spell 'come'."

Oh man! Was Andrew ready for this one! He stood proud, threw his shoulders back, held his head high, and the letters started tumbling out. All three of them:

"Ceeeeeeee — Uuuuuuuuuu — Mmmmmmmm!" said the proud

and confident young Andrew.

"Sit down please," urged the teachers, smothering their laughter.

To this day, Andrew doesn't understand why his spelling miscue has caused so much excitement. This incident did, though, provoke a good deal of discussion in the Skelton household. Belinda's brother suggested that Andrew should have asked the moderator to use the word in a sentence.

Who knows why, but Belinda just seems to attract bizarre happenings, be they comical or serious. Let's get to Belinda's tree.

Belinda purchased a lot in a subdivision for her new home, based solely on a beautiful giant hundred-year oak tree in the front yard. She and her husband even had the architect design the house around that tree. It was that spectacular.

Then, just weeks before she was to move in, it was time to hook up the electrical service. All utilities are underground in that subdivision, so the power company hired a contractor to dig a trench from the street to the power hookup for the house.

Dig a trench he did—right by the oak. Right by and *around* the oak—oh, about a foot away from the trunk. Belinda arrived home just as Mr. DitchWitch was finishing his work.

Horrified, she immediately started calling around to find an expert who could tell her how to save the tree from the damage to the root system done by the power company's contractor.

An arborist from the City of Atlanta showed up and immediately assessed the situation. First of all, the tree could not be saved. Second, it was in danger of falling at any time. Sadly, the tree was on the ground and in pieces in just a few hours—and Belinda's new home was standing there, designed around the memory of a giant oak.[22]

Mr. DitchWitch was still there watching the events unfold—and made the mistake of telling Belinda, "Calm down lady! It's

[22]Yes ... I know that this is what lawyers are for. Lawyers were called, and they did their job admirably. "Nuff said.

only a tree!" I'm told his recovery was long and painful.

Then there was Belinda's Christmas tree. This could only happen to Belinda.

She went out with hubby and the kids to select a nice Christmas tree, brought it home, set it up, strung the lights, put on the ornaments, and sat back to enjoy. The tree started moving. She was sitting there on the couch with the kids—and the tree was *moving*. Clark had run off on an errand, so she called me.

For some reason, she thinks I have all the answers.

Well, I didn't have the answer, so it was time to have some fun. I told her that there was probably a snake in the tree, and to get the kids out of the room and close the door until Clark got home. When Clark arrived to save the day, they found (to my surprise!) that there was no snake.

However, right at the bottom of the tree was a huge nest—a completely enclosed nest with just one little opening—and it was *moving*.

Pictures were taken and, the next day, wildlife experts were engaged to solve the mystery. It didn't take long to figure out that it was a flying squirrel nest. Belinda, her husband and the kids arrived back at home after another day's work and school, and the nest wasn't moving any more. The nest was removed and opened up.

Nothing. No flying squirrel. No squirrel in the nest, and none to be found in the house.

Belinda proposed the theory that it flew out an open door. A few days later, they noticed a smell—sort of a decomposing-rodent type of smell.

Now you have to know Belinda to understand that this was an absolute catastrophe! Belinda is, shall we say, a bit OCD. If you so much as touch a wall in her home, she will very likely have that wall repainted. She says that it "burnishes" the wall, whatever that means.

Now if this girl is going to repaint a wall because you place your hand on it, can you imagine how she reacted to a decaying squirrel in the house?

The smell did go away after a few days, but nothing was ever found. Somewhere in that house—and Belinda will find it at the worst possible time—is a tiny little flying squirrel skeleton.

That image and anticipation of the call she will make to me are sure to keep me grinning for years to come.

Did I tell you about the time Belinda told one of her sons—*in jest*, mind you—to walk up to some rough character on a Harley to deliver, shall we say, *a specific message*? Get ready.

The Harley had straight pipes and was impossibly loud as it roared into a parking space near Belinda's car. Belinda turned her back for a moment and, when she turned to say something else to Andrew, he was just a few feet away from the "biker."

"Andrew! No! Come back!"

Andrew waited until the biker removed his helmet. "Excuse me, sir, but is your bike so loud, because you're compensating for a small penis?"

Belinda couldn't hear the conversation, but she expected the worse.

"Andrew! Leave that man alone! Come here!"

The biker shot Belinda a glance, smiled, and just went about his business.[23]

There are many more Belinda stories out there than space allows and, after all, this book is about *me*!

But wait… there's…

CRISTINA GONZALEZ

In early 2006, a broadcasting acquaintance knew I was looking for a summer intern, and suggested that I might want to bring in the daughter of one of her friends. One look at her resume, and

[23]I'm with Belinda on this one. I ride motorcycles—quiet ones. Loud pipes just piss people off and make it rough on the rest of us. I truly wish they would start enforcing the noise ordinances on some of these guys.

I was persuaded, so Cristina came on board to handle whatever Belinda threw at her for a summer.

To put it bluntly, we were impressed. Cristina was absolutely one of the sharpest young ladies I had ever met. After she returned to school at New York University, we decided that we were going to do whatever it took to bring her on full time after she graduated.

Before then, she had one more internship to serve, so she spent that summer interning for my syndicator in New York City.

I'm not really sure just how but, in that capacity, she came to the attention of one Sean Hannity. *Uh oh.* It was looking like Sean and I were going to be locked into another battle—this time not over ratings, but over who got to hire Cristina after she picked up her diploma.

Clearly, I won that one. Cristina became a full-time part of the show in 2007.

I've never seen someone become so completely irreplaceable in such a short period of time. Here's a previously untold secret: You know those program notes that are posted every day to Boortz. com? Cristina started contributing to them as soon as she came on board. In a matter of weeks, she adapted to my writing style—not to mention my somewhat strange thought processes—and was turning out the bulk of Nealz Nuze.

Now she edits and produces large segments of the program for air—all in addition to keeping my feet to the fire. Cristina can hear what a talk show should sound like in her head.

It takes guts for a new hire to walk into the studio and say, "Look, Neal. You lost your focus in that last segment. When we come out of this next break, you need to find some point and hammer it home. The listeners aren't going to wait much longer."

Within a few years, Cristina will be a program director at a major talk radio station. Watch her—she's a star.

She's married to Matt Schaefer, an IT wizard and homemade beer bootlegger in Atlanta. He's a smart guy—but not as smart as his wife.

Cristina, by the way, is Cuban—a full-blooded, 100% Castrodespising Cuban. Her father came to this country from Cuba when he was 16, found a lovely Cuban lady, and in no time Cristina was on the scene.

Sometimes, you'll see Cristina wearing a chain around her neck with a key attached. That is the key to her grandfather's home in Havana—a home seized by Castro. Her dream is to return to Havana with that key and reclaim that property.

I would love to be there when she puts that key in the lock.

JAMIE DUPREE

Washington denizen Jamie Dupree is the national political correspondent for Cox Media Group. From his news booth, either on the Senate or the House side of the U.S. Capitol, Jamie covers political news for all of the Cox radio stations. For the first eight years of my show on *WSB*, Jamie was nothing more than a voice on our morning newscasts.

Then came 9/11.

I had been on the air the morning of September 11, 2001, for less than 30 minutes when the first airplane under the control of fanatic Islamic goons was flown into the World Trade Tower in New York City. I immediately exited the studio and turned the air over to the news people, including Jamie.

That night, I came on the air to do a few hours of talk with listeners eager to vent their anger and sorrow. Jamie joined me for that show, and we've been working together on the air every show since then.

Every broadcast day since 9/11, we've been doing a daily segment with Jamie dealing with political matters. Throughout this time, Jamie has managed to make liberals think that he is a conservative, and to make conservatives think he is liberal.

That would mean he has essentially been doing a perfect job.

Jamie is a child of Washington—he grew up there. His father was a lobbyist for Ford Motor Company. Before moving into journalism, Jamie worked as a page in the House of Representatives.

It's safe to say that Jamie Dupree is the go-to guy for dozens of correspondents with other broadcast and print outlets in Washington who are trying to chase down a story or to understand the machinations of the legislative branch of government.

Here's an oddity about Jamie: He never votes in presidential elections. This is a tribute to his impartiality. He feels that the very process of deciding which candidate to support in the election would cause him to form a bias that might sneak into his news coverage. Besides, no matter which way an election goes, Jamie will be able to say, "Don't look at me; I didn't vote for that idiot!"

Jamie doesn't know that I know, but several network and cable news operations have been snooping around him for quite some time. He's not biting, though, and we hope he continues resisting.

I've been the only radio talk show host with my very own national political correspondent in Washington DC. I've learned a lot from Jamie, and have truly enjoyed screwing with him on the air. He knows what I'm trying to do, though, and never takes the bait.

By the way, I've talked to a lot of people who have some rather strong suspicions that Jamie is actually part of some secret little intelligence cell inside the Beltway. He recently moved to a new home rather close to a place called Langley. He's a wiry little sonofabitch too, so it could certainly be possible.

He looks like Opie from the Andy Griffith Show—Opie with martial arts skills and a sidearm.

Ya just never know...

CLARK HOWARD

OK, Clark isn't really part of my *WSB* or syndication team, but I've been working together with him in radio longer than anyone else—since the *WGST* days.

Clark hosts a consumer-oriented radio talk show. He opens every show telling listeners that he will help them to save money and "avoid getting ripped off." Whether he's teaching someone how to save money on a cell phone bill or building a house, Clark is as good as they come.

There truly doesn't seem to be anything he doesn't know. He's also the author of many best-selling books on consumer and finance issues.

Clark is currently the co-anchor of the evening news show on HLN, sometimes known as Headline News and formerly known as CNN Headline news. He gets to work with people like Robin Meade, and for that we hate his everlasting guts.

Did I tell you Clark is tight? No?

OK, *Clark is tight*. This man probably does have the first dollar he ever earned. The stories of Clark's—let's be kind and call it frugality—are legendary and all true.

The Wendy's Hamburger

Let me set the scene:

Greg "Bugsy" Moceri, the *WSB* program director[24] takes Clark out to lunch. Clark decides they're going to eat at Wendy's. He does like himself some fast food. So Clark proceeds to purchase two single hamburgers—one loaded.

When he and Bugsy get to the table, Clark starts to take the two hamburgers apart. Bugs stops eating and just stares. There's Clark with two hamburger patties, two hamburger buns, some lettuce, tomatoes and the rest of the gunk spread all over his tray.

Once Clark has disassembled everything, he starts putting them back together, again. One hamburger bun is thrown away, and the two patties are then arranged with the cheese slices and the rest of the goodies in one bun.

Bugsy can't stand it any longer. "What in the HELL are you doing?"

Seriously, folks. I couldn't make this up. Clark then proceeds to tell Moceri that he just saved about 76 cents by purchasing two singles and combining them into one Wendy's double.

And guess what—*you know that now you're going to try the ex-*

---

[24]Now far and away the best talk radio consultant in the business.

act same thing!

Here's another:

Clark was visiting me in Naples. I took him to my club for dinner one evening. Clark then told me that he, too, is a member of a club in Naples, and he wanted to take me to lunch there the very next day.

Clark's "club" turned out to be the snack bar at Costco.

He won't overwhelm you with class. Just sayin.'

There is no consumer action exempt from Clark Howard's frugality. That includes car rentals and goes double for valet parking. He will park almost anywhere to avoid paying a valet—and, in New York City, if you're going to park at a hotel, *you're going to valet.*

So, on one occasion, Clark dropped his wife and luggage off at the hotel, and drove away in search of a place to park. Finally, about six blocks away, he found a place where he could wedge in the tiny little rental car.

So far, so good.

The next morning, he set out on his six-block walk to retrieve the car. There it was, under a pile of bricks. A building had partially collapsed overnight—crushing Clark's rental.

Gotta love it. Oh what I would have given to have seen the look on his face.

OK, one more Clark Howard story—my favorite:

Clark doesn't like to spend money on dry cleaning. Matter of fact, Clark doesn't like spending money on clothes at all. When you see him, chances are he's wearing a logo shirt given to him by one of his radio stations. If there's anything he hates more than *buying* clothes, it's having to pay to dry clean them. So Clark devised a scheme and, for years, has been working it pretty much to perfection.

There's this odd law in Georgia that says when you donate clothing to Goodwill or some other charity, the clothes must be washed or dry cleaned before they can be sold at a thrift store.

Clark did a few test runs. He would donate an article of clothing to Goodwill and then wait to see how long it took for that article to turn up at the thrift store. It didn't take him long to figure out that an article of clothing donated on, say, Monday would end up on the racks in the thrift store on Thursday or Friday.

You know where this is going, right?

To do his dry cleaning, Clark shows up at Goodwill with a nice donation on Monday. He then returns to go shopping on Thursday, when he will find his clothes and buy them back at about half the cost of dry cleaning them!

Sure, once in a while, someone will get to one of Clark's shirts before he does, but there are plenty of others from which to choose and, as I told you, Clark isn't exactly a clothes horse.

Pause.

I'll give you a few minutes to run to the next room and share that with someone. It's too funny to keep to yourself!

Now, while it's certainly fun to have a good laugh at some of Clark's antics and idiosyncrasies, this needs to be said: Clark Howard is possibly the most trusted public figure in Atlanta. Surveys and polling have repeatedly shown that he could be elected mayor.

He refuses to ever accept anything for free—not even a hotel room for a remote broadcast—over concerns it might affect his impartiality. Clark is a true icon in Atlanta, and would probably have retired long before now if his sense of duty to his listeners was not so strong.

As I write this, I am reminded yet again how blessed I have been to work over the years with so many wonderful people.

Belinda and Cristina are like sisters to me, and I'll do everything to maintain a close relationship with them long after retirement. We spend so much of our lives at work, and my life has been full in so many ways, because of these people who have been my second family.

THE SOUL OF THE BOORTZ TEAM... MY FAMILY

OK, so you've met my second family. Bet you didn't think you'd get to also meet my *first* family, did you? Today's your lucky day! Well, mine, actually—because I get to talk a bit here about the most important people in my life.

THE QUEEN

For a treat, this is the Donna chapter. Since my wife is a very private person, she didn't particularly want me to include this chapter in my book. I did, though, because I like to brag. I want you to realize what a lucky person I am.

I've mentioned that I'm writing this book as much for my grandbaby as I am for you, but there are things I only want to share with The Sprout[25], so I'll cover a good bit of it here, and leave the

---

[25] I used to refer to my daughter, Laura, as "Squirt." Still do, as a matter of fact. So calling her daughter "The Sprout" seemed like a natural. Beats "The Drip." That's anyone else's kid.

more private stuff in a letter that I'll slip into the book I put aside for her.

First, let me share a bit about Donna before I knew her. She grew up in Jacksonville, Florida, and she grew up poor. I don't mean living-in-a-one-bedroom, low-income-apartment-project poor—I mean *poor*.

Her father, who served in the Army Air Corps during World War II, abandoned his family when she was just 5 years old. He just got on his motorcycle and rode away. Donna and her brother moved with her mother into the garage behind her aunt's home in Jacksonville.

That's right, a garage. They hung clothes and sheets from ropes in the garage to separate the space into rooms. They had running water, a toilet and a shower, but no water heater. The running hot water came when she was 16 and preparing to leave home.

As soon as she was old enough, Donna started working to support her family. When her friends left Terry Parker High at the end of the day to play or hang around at each other's homes, Donna headed to the local movie theatre where she spent the evening selling popcorn and candy—often to her classmates who had come to see a movie.

Soon after graduation, Donna moved to Cape Canaveral. She got a job working at the Kennedy Space Center—and (she's going to kill me for saying this) did no small amount of partying with the astronaut crowd there. Sometime around 1966, Donna moved to Atlanta to live with an aunt and uncle in Cobb County.

That turned out to be a lucky move for me.

I'm not telling you all of this to generate sympathy. I'm telling you this to put some context into her journey to becoming the philanthropist she is today.

I met Donna in the fall of 1971 on a blind date, just a month or so after I separated from my first wife at the end of that not-all-that-pleasant five-year marriage.

The instigator here was a fellow WRNG talk show host by the name of Ben Baldwin. Ben and I had gone to an Atlanta Falcons football game and, on the way to his house for dinner afterward, he spilled the beans: "By the way, Carolyn has invited a friend of hers over to have dinner with us tonight. I think you'll like her."

I did.

Upon meeting me, Donna was, shall we say, completely and totally unimpressed.[26] After about three sentences out of my mouth, she looked at me and said, "You're an Aries, aren't you?"

"Why yes! How did you know?"

"It's obvious."

So if she was so unimpressed, why did she bother to say yes the first time I asked her out? Simple—and she'll admit it—she had a boyfriend she wanted to make jealous.

She knew just exactly where he was going to be on that particular evening, and she suggested we go there.

Sure! Why not?

At that time, I was living in a single's apartment complex called Riverbend. This was the era of the single's apartments, and Riverbend had recently been featured in a *Newsweek* magazine article about the phenomenon.

The place absolutely scared me to death, so when Donna told me to stay in my apartment and not go to the pool on a particular summer afternoon, because she was going to be there with her boyfriend (he was a bag buster at the Atlanta airport and also lived at Riverbend), I was happy to oblige.

I know. What a *wuss*.

It was a war—of attrition—and I won. I beat the bag buster. She tells me that a turning point was one evening when she told me she was thinking of moving to Dallas. She noticed a tear in my eye. It's true. I couldn't hide it—the prospect of her moving away saddened me more than I expected it would.

One day in 1973, I proposed to her in the parking lot of the Lovable Bra Company where she was working. How very romantic. I told her I had two tickets to Hawaii (a radio station promo-

---

[26]A somewhat normal occurrence among most of the people I met in the early 70s.

tion) and asked her if she would like to go.

She said she would, and I told her that the only way she was going to make that trip with me would be if it was our honeymoon. Again, how romantic.

We got married (this time my parents wholeheartedly approved—not that it would have made any difference) and the next morning we were off to Waikiki.[27] Outrigger Hotel, in case you want to know, home of the Perry Brothers Smorgy. Right across the street from The International Marketplace. A wonderful honeymoon.

Yes, I have many wonderful stories about Donna. But she is a *very* private person. She is not one bit fond of the public recognition that comes with my job. Donna has only listened to me on the radio once in the 40 years that I've known her, and that is right after she met me. She said she almost ran off the road listening to my "crap," as she called it. That one statement will win her even more fans.

It didn't stop her from going out with me, though, because—remember—she had a boyfriend to make jealous.

Recognizing and honoring Donna's penchant for privacy, I'll just reveal a few details. She worked hard to support our family while I was going to law school and then served as my legal secretary during the first years of my practice. Her experience working with other high-powered law firms was invaluable.

Later, she owned and operated her own travel agency. She spent years working for The Friendship Force, a citizen exchange group begun by President Jimmy Carter and Rev. Wayne Smith. But

---

[27]Golly! There's a story I want to tell you about that flight to Hawaii, but I don't want it to mess up the narrative about The Queen, so I'll put it into this footnote. I did something on that United 747 flying across the Pacific that would get me arrested today. No, not *that*. You see, there was a tourist-class lounge on that airplane. In that lounge was a table full of snacks: potato chips, candies, cheeses—and fortune cookies. I took one of those fortune cookies back to my seat and very carefully pulled the fortune out. I then tore another piece of paper into the same shape, wrote a message on it, and stuffed it back into the cookie. I put the cookie back into the bowl. The message? "This plane will never make it to Hawaii." Not very nice, I know.

Donna really came into her own when she started giving money away.

I've written five books. This is the sixth. Three of those books have been on *The New York Times Bestseller's List*. One debuted at Number One. The other two started in second place. You can earn some big bucks writing bestselling books, and every penny—I mean every *single* penny—that I have earned from those books has gone to Donna's private foundation, *The Donna Boortz Foundation*.

She has a group of scouts, her Board of Directors, who look for individuals in desperate circumstances. Donna and her board then study these individuals. They look at how they fell upon hard times, what they're trying to do to help themselves, what obstacles they face, and what type of help they need. That help could be anything from buying someone a car to paying a few months' rent or utilities—even getting them a set of teeth!—to get them past a rough spot.

Donna's foundation is not the type that donates money to groups or organizations. She looks for the individual in trouble and gives that helping hand. Donna is also a lifetime member of the Tiffany Circle of the Red Cross. This is a lady that truly knows, and has taught me, the absolute joy that comes from reaching out to help someone in a truly tough spot.

Her business card for her foundation has a depiction of an angel. When I look at that card, I see her.

OK, I've invaded her privacy enough here. I could tell you of some of the wonderful things that Donna has done for people—specific examples. But she takes the biblical admonition of "Go and tell no man" seriously. She's in this to help people, not for the recognition. Every single penny of expenses for the operation of her foundation comes out of her pocket. Every single penny donated to her foundation is spent helping people.

I know what you're thinking.

"Someone like this is married to a jerk like you?"

Don't think for a minute I don't wonder about that myself.

Without Donna, I wouldn't have any friends. Simple as that.

Donna also has a passion for travel, as do I, and right around the end of January of 2013, we're hitting the roads, the skies and the seas. I know that no matter where in the world we are, she's going to have that foundation checkbook with her and a constant ear tuned to her scouts in Naples and Atlanta.

There's always someone who could benefit from a little helping hand. Don't bother trying to find her, by the way. If you're the next person her foundation will help, they'll find you.

SQUIRT

That's the nickname I've always had for our daughter, Laura.

Again, Laura is a very private person. I think she was somewhat secretly relieved when she got married (a wonderful guy, by the way) and could start using her married name, rather than going around with that "Boortz" thing hanging around her neck.

Trust me, it doesn't always help.

Having to get by the ol' "Are you any relation to… " thing in your professional life can get quite old. So Laura would just as soon be left out of this, but there are some things I just have to say about her.

First, she loves animals. She absolutely loves all living things. I remember one time when she was about 14 years old, she found a wounded squirrel in our driveway. I think the squirrel had become involved in an altercation with a cat. At any rate, she took the squirrel and wrapped it in a warm towel.

The squirrel soon expired—off to the squirrel dirt nap—so Laura left it and the towel on the bathroom counter. That evening, I went into the bathroom to brush my teeth and wash my face. I picked up the towel to dry my face—and the scream could be heard throughout the house.

Who, after all, likes to dry their face with a dead squirrel?

Soon after meeting her husband to be, she found out that he was an expert competitive shooter. She had no problem with that at all, but did ask him if he ever hunted—if he ever shot animals. He told her he did not. She told him that this was a good thing, because it would be an absolute and unqualified deal-breaker.

In the early years of my talk radio career, Laura would accompany me to the studios on holidays. The listeners grew fond of listening to her do the show with me on Thanksgiving mornings. This caused problems for me, because she sounded a good bit smarter and a whole lot more compassionate than I did.

Compassionate? She would have made a lousy talk show host.

Let me tell you what an impressive young lady she was: In the summers, while her high school classmates spent their days at the lake or hung around the mall, Laura went a few hundred miles south of Atlanta to Cordele, Georgia. There, she served as a counselor at Camp Civitan, a summer camp operated at a state park near there for children with disabilities. These kids loved her, but not nearly as much as she loved them.

She took this love of helping people with her to Georgia Southern University, where she majored in recreational therapy. She then continued at Georgia State to get a Masters degree.

Today, she has more initials after her name than any doctor I know, and works as a rehab specialist for a large company in the insurance industry. She travels around Georgia, helping to devise rehab career guidance and life plan programs for the disabled and people who have been injured or sidelined with illnesses.

I couldn't be prouder of her. She will scream when she sees I've included her in this book.

Hey, Sprout! That's your Mama I'm talking about!

SPROUT

That's my granddaughter. I'm telling you absolutely nothing about her, except to say that she is just about the smartest and cutest 3-1/2 year old little girl you have ever seen in your life. She loves all of the Disney princesses, and can give you the names and histories of all of them.

The Queen and I fully intend to do everything we can to completely and utterly spoil this little girl, and then let her parents deal with the consequences. As long as I have a dollar left to my name, and her parents agree, of course, that little girl will not spend one single day being emotionally and intellectually abused in a government school.

You do know why grandparents get along so well with their grandchildren, don't you? They share a common enemy.

Enough about my family.

As I said, they are very private people, and beyond what I've said here, I intend to keep them for myself.

MY JOB AS A TALK SHOW HOST WAS TO...

I covered this in *Somebody's Gotta Say It* but, going on the assumption that most of the people reading this didn't necessarily buy that book five years ago, I'm going to cover it again, here.

I've had a 42-year career, but doing what? Changing the world? Having a profound effect on American politics? Forty-two years providing a sounding board for people with telephones—and later cellphones—who wished to opine on the qualities of our president or the failings of Michael Vick? Forty-two years helping to steer our Republic down the path of enlightenment and righteousness?

No. *Hardly*.

The brutal truth of the matter is that I spent 42 years trying to get people to listen to commercials on radio stations.

I started out my career as a disc jockey. Playing records.[28] I ended my career playing callers.

To people with an advanced education and capable of understanding complex issues, I was known as a radio talk show host.

To bed-wetting left-wingers, proggies, Democrats, ObamaBots (getting redundant here), the mainstream media, pretty much anyone who works for CNN, voids surrounded by sphincter muscles, footstools and Democrats, I was known as a preacher of hate[29], and what I did wasn't talk radio—it was "hate" radio.

Some may think, and I dare say that most of my colleagues in the talk radio industry might agree, that my purpose in doing the show is to present and win converts to a certain political ideology. Perhaps I was on the radio for some particular political candidate or proposition.

Wrong.

Again, here's the truth: My job description was simple. I was supposed to be interesting and compelling enough for about 38 minutes out of every hour to attract listeners from certain pre-defined demographic groups—people who certainly had other things to do—and to then keep them listening long enough to be there the next time I said "we'll be back" to make time for some commercials.

It was a bonus if I could be entertaining enough for the listeners to actually stay there and absorb the information in those commercials, so that they would be around when the commercials were over. I would then be charged with keeping their attention for a few more minutes, so that we could start the whole routine all over, again.

The formula is simple: The longer folks listen, the more com-

---

[28]Records—you know, round, shiny flat things. Usually black, with a label in the middle. Records have grooves on them. Two, to be exact. When you put a tiny little needle in one of those grooves, and then turn the plastic thingy, the shape of the grooves will cause the needle to vibrate. If you hook the needle up to some wires connected to electronic stuff— vacuum tubes, when I started—the vibrations can be turned into noise. Noise like "Wooly Bully," which would then cause you to take the shiny black round thing and run over it with your Rambler. This is where the word "groovy" came from.

[29]The purpose of the word "hate," as with the word "racist," is to halt conversation. The words are not used to define a principle or philosophy or even an emotion. They are used to shut down conversation. Period. That's it. "You're full of hate; therefore, I don't need to listen to anything you say." There. See how easy that is?

mercials they hear. The more commercials they hear, or the more people who hear the commercials, the more stuff they buy from the advertisers, and the more money the advertisers make. That gives them more money to spend on advertising, which means the radio stations will make more money and some of that money will end up in my pocket.

That's it. That's my job. That is the essential truth about the talk show host.

I'm not there to change the world. I'm not there to create social upheaval. I'm not there to get one politician elected or another defeated. Sure, I have my opinions, and expressed those opinions. But like anyone else on the radio, I'm there to keep you, the listener, interested enough to stay tuned until the time comes for us to play the next block of commercials. Some jocks do it with music. I'm one of those who do it with ideas.

With luck, if I've done my job, as I've already said, you'll even be interested enough to sit through that commercial break while I catch my breath, then listen to me for another few minutes, so I can then play even more commercials.

Are you getting the point here?

Good, because I've never heard another talk radio host admit any of this to his audience. Nor do I expect this to happen. Perhaps it's more fun, or more fulfilling, to believe that you're part of—dare I say the *leader* of—some great crusade for God, motherhood, blue skies, green lights and golden sunsets across a beautiful lake or misty mountains for every American ever born than to consider yourself highly paid filler inserted between commercials.

I was more than happy with my role in our business community doing what I do—help people sell stuff. And judging from the number of people who approach me in public, I gather a few of you would like to take over when I retire.

"I'm hoping to get in the business. I want to be a radio talk show host!" they say. "What can you tell me?"

You want to be a talk show host? Really?

Well, first of all, let me tell you: I don't have a clue as to how to determine who will and will not be an effective and successful talk show host. I've seen people with every imaginable credential try this stuff, and fall flat on their faces. I've seen others you could only laugh at walk into a studio, and then come out a few hours later well on their way to a new, and rather odd, career.

If you want to give this a try, my best piece of advice is to move to a small radio market and get a job doing anything they'll let you do at the local talk station. Sure, that's what they told me and I ignored it to tackle a large radio market. Lightning struck for me, but I'm guessing it flashes more often where the competition for openings isn't so fierce.

Sooner or later, you can weasel yourself into a weekend slot, then maybe a daily show. Keep plugging away at it.

Now, if you're really determined to try this thing, two very important points:

The very first day I walked into the studios of *WRNG* Radio in Atlanta to visit Herb Elfman, I noticed a poster on the wall over the receptionist's desk. There was a drawing of a man in thought, his chin resting on his hands. To the side were these words uttered in 1874 by John Viscount Morley:

"You have not converted a man because you have silenced him."

To this day, I have not seen that poster or those words posted in any other talk station or studio I have visited over 42 years. That's a shame. Those words registered on me the very first time I saw them, and they should be posted in every talk studio in the country.

Silence more often indicates contemplation, not defeat, but you can't wait around while a caller stews and contemplates—so, by necessity, it's off to the next one.

The second point—one that my colleagues in the industry are more than sick to death of hearing from me—is this:

They're not followers.

They're listeners.

That should be easy to understand. Yet it has been my observation that, as a talk show host, once you've reached the point where you believe those listeners out there are ready to follow you into hell, you may look over your shoulder one day and find yourself marching alone.

You're there to entertain these people, not to lead them. Sure, we talk politics. Maybe you'll even change some minds out there. That's great. Good for you.

But ask your station owner if he's thrilled that you changed some folks' minds on some political issues. He only cares whether or not you entertained them in the process. If you want to lead them, the boss wants you to lead them to your advertisers' doors.

I know that this just doesn't sit well with many of my colleagues—and I'm sorry for that. If you want to lead, get into politics, write a book, or get your flute and start walking through a Democrat neighborhood. See how many of them you can get to follow you to a raging river somewhere.

There. Just that simple. And, thank you, my friends, for listening to those commercials, heading to those advertisers, and buying their stuff.

Thanks to you, I was able to run from the law 20 years ago.

THE PUBLIC'S AIRWAVES

Wanna hear one of the most asinine absurdities ever uttered in connection with any discussion at any time in any location relating to broadcasting—radio and TV—in the United States?

That would be the bogus idea that we broadcasters are utilizing "the public's airwaves" for our shows, whether the shows is news, entertainment or commentary.

Get real.

How did this absurdity come about?

Simple: *The Quest For Power.*

Can anyone doubt that, if broadcasting—radio, TV and, yes, the Internet, by the way—had been around when our founders wrote the Bill of Rights, they would have included all of these methods of communication in the First Amendment?

The very purpose behind protecting the freedom of the press from government intrusion was to ensure that the politically powerful could not use the police power of government to interrupt or to affect the flow of information to and among citizens.

Think about that.

This free flow of information was seen as key to preserving freedom and holding government and politicians in check. Back then, there were only two ways to convey information: You either wrote it or you said it.[30]

There you have the reason why writing your message (freedom of the press) or saying it (freedom of speech) are both protected in our Constitution:

They included every method of disseminating information there was to protect—at that time.

Now think back on all the times you've read or seen or heard news reports about some coup or revolution in another country. How many times did you read or hear the reporter say that the rebels have seized control of laundromats, car dealerships or Pilates studios?

Never, right?

Instead, you hear reports that the rebels have seized control of the radio and TV stations and the newspapers. When you are preparing to take over a government, or moving to deny the people their basic liberties, your first task is to get control of the means by which information—news—is distributed.

OK, maybe that's your second task. The first task may be making the current leader disappear—usually under a few feet of dirt, unless you have a large body of water, some chains, and an anchor to spare.

Here's something else to think about: Years ago, before the Internet age, the majority of Americans got their news and information from radio and TV. If you had a job, you were listening to the radio on the way to work. No job? You may have been watching

---

[30]Well, there were paintings on the walls of caves. That would be because these artists weren't all that handy with the tools of literature, and you could only convey so much information through grunts.

the morning shows on TV. It was a similar story in the evenings. Before the Internet, most people got their evening news from TV newscasts.

Newspapers? They played a vital role, but only to a minority of news consumers. Now less than 25 percent of Americans read a daily paper. That's a sad statistic, and I wish that it were not so, but that's the reality. The trends today are increasingly away from newspapers and magazines.

Newsweek magazine announced in July of 2012 that it was going to cease printing weekly copies of the magazine and publish only on the Internet. Today, most Americans get their political news— and that's the type of news we're concerned with here—from the Internet, then from radio and TV, with the minority getting their news from printed media.

So, consider this: In a nation founded by people who saw fit to include freedom of the press in the very first item of the Bill of Rights, most people are now getting their news and information from either entities that are already licensed by the state (radio and TV) or from entities that politicians are absolutely falling over each other to reign in and control (the Internet).

As you read this, there are people working within the United Nations to affect international control—and that includes content control—over the Internet and to levy a tax on users. Sadly, we have politicians in this country who are supportive of that effort and, for the most part, they put "Ds" after their names when they identify themselves.

It's just this simple: Politicians love power, and despots love power exponentially more. Control over the dissemination of information is rightfully seen as a key to maintaining power, and that's where this "public's airwaves" absurdity came from.

Step back a second.

I've already asked if you have any doubts at all that our founding fathers would have included broadcasting in the First Amendment if radio had been a reality at the time.

Of course they would have.

Let's turn the tables. What if the Bill of Rights was being written right now? Do you think our present-day political class would write a clause granting absolute protection of the freedoms that the printed media enjoys today? You do? You can't be serious.

Almost 100 years *after* the birth of our country, some lady in Italy downloaded an infant by the name of Guglielmo Marconi. I'm not going to turn this into a history lesson, but suffice it to say that this Italian was later credited with the invention of radio—a way to transmit information across vast distances through the air without wires or cables.

Again, no history lesson, but you need to think about this: As the popularity of radio grew, the political class did what all political classes eventually do—they moved to regulate this new medium.

Let's face it. Politicians greeted the arrival of radio with more worry than wonderment. Here was a means of spreading information not only to vast numbers of people, but to vast numbers of people who can't even read!

To make matters far worse, the information could be shared instantly! Stories of political misdeeds in Washington could spread throughout the country in a matter of hours, instead of days or weeks. Political errors and misjudgments would be more difficult to contain once every American with a pulse and access to a new-fangled radio heard about them.

Sad to say but, by the time broadcasting arrived on our doorstep, the love of freedom and preservation of the liberties of the people were not what you would call foremost on the minds of politicians.

Then as now, the acquisition and maintenance of political power came first.

Whatever came second was far, far behind. It was clear: This radio thing had to be brought under control, and sooner rather than later.

On what pretext, though, could the Imperial Federal Government of the United States seize control over broadcasting?

Well, let's noodle this one out, shall we? The signals somehow fly through the air, and everybody has a right to their share of the air, don't they? After all, if you're denied air, you die! All God's chill'ren gotta breathe!

That must mean that everyone owns the air and, if that's true, then it's reasonable for them to expect their wonderful elected officials to control what flies through that air—whether it's old-time radio dramas like *The Green Lantern* or modern-day talk show hosts like Rush Limbaugh. You certainly wouldn't want to allow someone to interfere with the very air that people depend on for their very lives!

Brilliant!

If the people own the airwaves, the people get to say what can and cannot be broadcast there! And, of course, they'll do that through their elected officials!

Presto. With the absurd theory of "the public's airwaves," the power of broadcasting was now officially controlled by the government.

I'm not suggesting, mind you, that there was no need for regulation in broadcasting. Proponents of the government's role in regulating broadcasting point to the scarcity of available broadcast frequencies and the resulting need to regulate the use of those frequencies as the primary excuse for the existence of the Federal Communications Commission.

I'm sorry, but that reasoning just doesn't stand up to the test. Broadcast frequencies aren't the only thing limited out there—so is land! Yet our founding fathers didn't see fit to create a government bureaucracy with the mandate to regulate land use by private individuals and to make sure that land was all used "in the public interest," as they have with broadcast frequencies.

Is your head hurting, yet? Hang with me here.

If broadcasting had been around when our Bill of Rights was being crafted, there is little doubt that our founders would have limited regulation to simply protect one broadcaster's right to their particular broadcast frequency without interruption or interference from another—in much the same way our rights in land are protected today.

If you try to build a structure on your neighbor's land, the law will stop you. If you use your land in a way that interferes with your neighbor's use of his land, the law will stop you.

That, my friends, should be the limited role of government in the regulation of broadcasting: Don't interfere with someone else's use of their frequency—the law will stop you.

So how in the world did these frequencies come to be privately owned? How did I come to own the website known as Boortz. Com?

Well, I created it and registered it. Pretty simple concept. We also have government auctioning off new broadcasting spectrums all the time. When you buy one of those frequencies, it should be yours. Period. End of saga.

And the government should be there to protect your property right. It is no longer "the public's airwaves"—it's *yours*.

There is far more space in the airwaves for the transmission of information than there is on the shelves of the nation's bookstores. Yet books are protected from the heavy hand of government. Information transmitted through the air is not.

The airwaves are considered to belong to the public *only* because our founding fathers didn't know they existed, so they couldn't include them in the First Amendment—just as they couldn't have envisioned personal computers or Xerox machines back when they were knocking out copies of the Constitution and its amendments in pen and ink.

Is that so hard to fathom?

In 1776, air was for breathing, blowing up balloons and flying kites—not much else. For all I know, they didn't even have balloons then, so that was a guess. If Thomas Jefferson and his buddies had foreseen the era of broadcasting, there's no doubt that First Amendment protections would have been guaranteed for radio and television.

I don't mean to belabor this, but I'm not through hammering on this "public's airwaves" nonsense, yet. It's a big issue that affects you in a big way, whether you pay attention or not.

Question: Just what did you do to claim any ownership over these airwaves? Where is your claim of title? These broadcast frequencies have been developed or discovered by the private sector, not by government.

Here's the deal in a nutshell: Those in power—yes, politicians— know how important it is to control the flow of information. As it became glaringly apparent that most of the information was or soon would be flowing over the airwaves, they had to create a fiction in order to exercise their control. That fiction is that the airwaves belong to the people.

As technology has evolved, it has become obvious that much— perhaps *most*—of this information is flowing over the Internet. Their reaction? They broadened the role of the FCC to ensure that everyone has their "right" to Internet access, *thus setting the stage for control of that medium as well.*

Open your eyes. This is not rocket science.

In all of this, you'll continue to find the "scarcity" excuse. "Well, we have to exercise this control, because of the scarcity of available frequencies."

Nonsense. With advancing technology, scarcity is virtually non-existent.

Politicians and various activists on both sides of the political spectrum use this "public's airways" fiction to pursue their goal of controlling the dissemination of information.

Do you seriously believe that other countries are the only ones who want to tightly control what the masses learn about government practices?

Richard Nixon was adept at using the so-called "fairness doctrine," in an attempt to shut down broadcast critics of his antics in office. In recent years, with the popularity of conservative talk radio, leftists have called for a renewal of the fairness doctrine to shut down people like Rush Limbaugh.

OK, take a break. Deep breaths. Knee bends. Stretch.

This last part is important, and I want you to be alert.

In order for radio and TV stations to deliver their news as information to you, they have to use the "public's airwaves," right? This is all the excuse needed for the government to regulate radio and TV stations by making them operate according to some politician's view of what the "public interest" is, right?

Do you see the scary writing on the wall?

How is a newspaper, news magazine or book going to make it into your hands without traveling over the public's roads and highways? Heck, not only that, but you actually paid for those roads and highways out of your own pocket through various forms of taxation, didn't you? So, by definition, those are the public's roads and highways, right?

Well, doesn't that mean that the government can regulate the newspapers that are dependent on the public's roads and highways for distribution? Shouldn't the government step in and demand that these newspapers and magazines operate "in the public interest?" Maybe the government should issue licenses to these printed publications, and threaten non-renewal to those who fall on the wrong side of certain political issues, or who simply aren't politically correct enough. You don't think that argument holds water? Then pray tell, my proggie friends, just what is the conceptual difference here?

Government can regulate radio and TV content, because they use the public's airwaves, but not newspaper, magazine and other printed content, even though they use the public's roads and highways?

You get it now, don't you?

The only reason most Americans get their news and information from outlets controlled by the government (true) is because our politicians upon the advent of broadcasting and the Internet are far less dedicated to the idea of liberty and freedom (true) than were the people who founded this country and wrote the documents of our heritage.

Our mission, should we choose to accept it—*and we should, if we are to restore and preserve America's greatness*—is to protect the legacy of freedom given us by our ancestors. This means we must remain informed and fight for freedom of communications in all its forms.

To do any less is a betrayal of the people who formed this government as one that *protects* rights, not one that grants and limits them.

For 42 years, I've been proud to be a part of a talk radio industry that has been providing to Americans information that is often intentionally ignored by the rest of the media.

The left, for obvious reasons, wants to fight talk radio—but how?

I've already mentioned it, remember? The Fairness Doctrine. And they might sound harmless, but there's something new on the horizon: community advisory boards.

Go run around in the rain, play with your kids, remember why you care—and come back ready to learn.

IF YOU CAN'T BEAT 'EM, DESTROY 'EM.

Talk radio doesn't work all that well for liberals, but it's terrific for conservatives and Libertarians, who dominate the airwaves.

So it is, so it shall always be, right?

Not so fast.

The future of talk radio depends upon just who has a grip on the machinery of the federal government. If Republicans control it, talk radio is essentially safe—and why not? The successful shows mostly sing Republican refrains.

But, should the White House and Congress stay in the hands of the Democrats, you can expect a move against talk radio.

Think about it. Why shouldn't they try to destroy an element of the media that certainly isn't friendly to their goals or philosophy?

They have a couple of options.

One, of course, is to resurrect the so-called "Fairness Doctrine."

The other, which I'll also address, is a somewhat newer idea involving community review or oversight boards. I made my living in talk radio for over four decades. You can guess that I'm very fond of the medium, and feel very protective toward it.

I can't wrap up my time with you on the airwaves without detailing these two threats to talk radio, those who learn from it and the people who want to make it their career.

The Fairness Doctrine

You really have to love the way politicians attach feel-good names to regulations or legislation that makes you do anything but feel good. One of my favorites is an oldie called "The Bank Secrecy Act."

Now you might think that this legislation was passed to make your bank accounts safe from prying eyes. It's your business, right?

Actually, the purpose of the law was to open your bank account to the prying eyes of the federal government. Just one of the provisions of that Act requires your bank, without notifying you, to report to the IRS any cash deposit or withdrawal into or out of your checking or savings account in the amount of $10,000 or more.[31]

How's that for secrecy?

OK, so the "fairness" word was attached to this attempt to reign in broadcasting. That makes it just fine, right?

Here's what the libs will tell you about The Fairness Doctrine: They'll say that the only thing they are trying to do is to make sure all sides of an issue are presented on "the public's airwaves."

Now that just sounds so immensely wonderful and FAIR, don't you think?

Question: Why aren't newspapers required to present all sides of an issue or argument?

Oh! Darn, almost forgot. Newspapers are *protected by the First*

---

[31]This is one of the reasons we'll never get rid of this asinine war on drugs in this country. The government loves to tell us that they have to spy on our bank accounts to spot drug trafficking. Bolshoi. They just love to track our money—to make sure they've seized as much as they can get away with.

Amendment. Broadcasters, though most people get their news today through radio and TV, are not.

As I pointed out in the last chapter, most people in this country rely on entities *that are licensed to operate by the federal government* for their news.

Are you comfy with that?

Forget this "fairly present all sides" farce. *Gimme a break.*

I can tell you how the Fairness Doctrine would work in real life if the liberals were ever able to put this absurd law on the books, again.

Remember, the primary targets of the progs with the Fairness Doctrine would be right-wing syndicated talk show hosts. We're primarily talking about Rush Limbaugh and Sean Hannity. Sure, they would like to take out the others, but Hannity and the Godfather would be their key targets.

These politicians are not stupid, after all. *Just idiotic.*

So here's how it would work: Hannity has about 500 stations, Limbaugh 600. As soon as The Fairness Doctrine is back in play, some leftist organization—Media Matters or MoveOn.org each come to mind—would appoint monitors to listen to the Big Shots.

These monitors—liberal hacks, all—will wait until Sean or Rush expresses an opinion on some controversial matter. Then a coordinated campaign will begin to get local members of these organizations to write letters to their affiliate radio stations, demanding equal time to respond to evil conservative words uttered by Sean or Rush on the air.

A copy of the letter will be sent to the FCC. The station, fearing an enforcement action that will result in a fine or worse from the FCC, will quickly relent and make time available to the proggie activist to come on the station and present an opposing viewpoint.

The trick is that this doesn't just happen *once.*

While one MoveOn or Media Matters stooge is pursuing their equal time shot, another is tuning in to find some issue on which *they* will demand *their* equal time. Within weeks, if not days, every local Limbaugh or Hannity affiliate will be faced with a deluge of demands for equal time on the air.

It's only "fair," right?

In no time, the requests could easily number into the hundreds.

Well, of course it would be impossible for the station to honor all of these requests and still broadcast anything an audience would reasonably be expected to enjoy.

The stations are then faced with a choice: If they keep the syndicated talk shows, they'll continue to be overwhelmed with logistics of satisfying the equal-time requests. The only reasonable solution for station management will be to drop the syndicated shows and go to strictly local programming.

Mission accomplished.

Limbaugh and Hannity are vanquished, along with pretty much every other syndicated talk show.

There's a problem, though. Federal courts have made it plain that they don't particularly like the Fairness Doctrine, and Congress has already shouted down the idea once. With congressional disapproval, it would be hard for the FCC, even under Obama, to reinstitute the Fairness Doctrine. The Democrats may still have the White House and the Senate, but the good guys are in the driver's seat in the House, so the Fairness Doctrine is dead—for now.

Maybe Obama could try it through Executive Order. He seems to believe that there are no limits to his power in this regard, but it's more likely that some other tactic has to be developed.

But not to fear, liberal friends! There's an alternative solution out there!

These ideas have been around for about 30 years now, but have gained renewed popularity under Obama. Here's the game plan:

1. Shorten the license renewal period from eight to four years, possibly three.
2. Require that a certain percentage of each station's primetime broadcast day be locally produced.
3. Activate community advisory boards.

These are all things that could presumably be done by the FCC without the bothersome chore of enacting any legislation. So here is how *this* works:

The whole scheme will be wrapped into the idea that these radio stations need to broadcast "in the public interest," since they are using "the public's airwaves."

To ensure the public's interest is being met, the FCC will first shorten the license renewal procedure to four, possibly three years. This will keep station owners and managers on their toes and constantly aware that their entire business could be taken away from them all too quickly.

Then the FCC steps in with their "locally produced" rules. The number that has been tossed around is 25 percent, but 25 percent of what? Certainly, the rules would not permit stations to make their local hours between midnight and 6 a.m. The rules would require that the bulk of the "local" time be during prime listener hours. This means stations would have to dump a syndicated host during prime hours.

Who would be the first to go? Levin? Hannity? Rush?

Can't be me. I'm going away, anyway.

Then comes the real gem: Community Advisory Boards.

These boards would be selected by local politicians and community "activists." Most of the talk radio listeners are in larger cities, and most of these larger cities are pretty much controlled by Democrats, so you can figure out what these advisory boards will look like. When the station owners apply every couple of years for their license renewals, the FCC will look to these advisory boards for a recommendation as to whether or not the renewal should be granted.

In the interim, the members of these boards would be constantly harassing, if you will, these stations about their broadcast content.

"You're carrying all conservative talk hosts. You're not meeting the needs of this community. When are you going to put a liberal on the air?"

You get the drift.

Station owners, fearing for their licenses, will genuflect before the almighty advisory boards—and conservative shows will hit the road. The beauty is that this bullying tactic can be used against local as well as syndicated hosts! You cut back on the syndicated hosts with the "localism" rule, and then cut back conservative opinion further with the advisory boards.

Pretty slick, huh?

And it's all possible, because of this "public's airwaves" scam and the urgent desire of the politically powerful to control the dissemination of information wherever and whenever they can.

This scheme for shutting down conservative talk radio would, of course, be pretty much dead in the water had Obama failed to win a second term. Bear in mind, though, that should conservatives someday rule in Washington to the degree that liberals do today, accompanied by a rise in liberal talk radio, these same tactics can be used to shut down the left.

So there you have it folks: *So much for freedom of the "press" and freedom of expression.* Despots love to control the flow of information—and there is no shortage of despots among us.

WHY LIBERALS SUCK AT TALK RADIO

When I began my talk radio career with *WRNG* in Atlanta, there was a fairly even mix of liberals and conservatives on the Ring Radio team. I was the hard-right guy, and a veteran TV newsman by the name of Bill Conover held down center right. A very interesting radio veteran named Ben Baldwin (the man who introduced me to Donna) was center left, and two unforgettable Peabody-Award-winning blondes[32] named Mickie (Silverstein) and Teddy (Levison) held down the far-left portion of our broadcast day.

That was about as balanced a talk radio lineup I've ever seen on any talk station—and it didn't last.

As I continued through my four decades behind the mic, I saw

---

[32]Don't give me any flack on my calling them blondes. They referred to themselves as "Golden Retrievers," so I don't think they would mind.

liberal shows fail one after the other, while conservative or Libertarian shows flourished. Sure, they tried liberal hosts. But they usually failed.

When I made the move to *WGST*[33], they had a most interesting liberal character on the air named Tom Houck[34]. Houck had dropped out of high school in the 1960s to join the Civil Rights Movement. He eventually became Dr. Martin Luther King Jr.'s driver. Connections? Nobody had 'em like Tom Houck. Connections and experiences aside, he was a liberal and, as a liberal, he was all but doomed as a talk show host.

After a few years, his show was over.

So, why is this? Why do liberals—even liberals with some rather remarkable credentials and amazing histories—end up failing at talk radio?

Glad you asked.

I happen to have the answer. I first covered this in *Somebody's Gotta Say It*. It's even truer now than it was then.

People who listen to talk radio have some of the most finely tuned bullshit detectors you'll find anywhere. They can smell a phony right through the radio dial, and that's exactly where they head when they detect one—to the dial to change stations. Talk radio listeners will accept and tolerate any position on any issue, if it's presented with honesty, rationality and just the smallest dose of logic. They'll also tolerate irrational and illogical banter, if it's presented with a good dose of humor.

Let's recap: What are the listeners looking for? Honesty, ratio-

---

[33]Sad to say, the demise of WGST as a talk station occurred on September 1, 2012. On that day, Rush Limbaugh moved to WSB in Atlanta and WGST started reporting soccer scores in Spanish. Know what? They shouldn't have offered me a cut in pay when my contract expired in 1992.

[34]There are great stories to be told about pretty much everyone I've known in talk radio. There's one on Tom Houck I can't let pass. We were doing, for some now-unexplainable reason, a remote broadcast for the opening of The Gold Club. Yup, a strip joint. Tom was sitting at the table with about three... er... strippers. Noticing their, shall we say, accoutrements, Houck said, "I can see you've all had breast altercations, right? That's true, right? You've all had breast altercations." I want a ringside seat for *that* bout.

nality and logic? Failing that, at least some humor?

All this means is that liberals are pretty much screwed when it comes to success in talk radio. It's clear that the facts are working against them, and they can't carry an argument using logic or reason. As far as a sense of humor is concerned... well, let me know how your search for a truly funny liberal turns out.[35]

Liberals are very successful in the printed media. They're also successful in what is commonly, though erroneously, referred to as TV journalism. There's a reason for this and I'm about to 'splain it to you.

Let's consider two hypothetical liberals: One is a newspaper columnist, the other a talk show host. We'll have these two proggies address an issue of great importance and interest—like gun control—to the public. We'll get the liberal columnist and talk show host together and write a quick essay on the need for more stringent gun control measures.

The columnist has his piece published in 100 newspapers. The talk show host offers the very same words as his opinion at the beginning of his show, which is heard on 100 radio stations. We'll give our newspaper friend a break and assume that his opinions are being read by the same number of people who might be listening to the liberal speaker.

So what happens after the liberal columnist and talk show host have each had their say? Thousands of liberals who read the column agreed with every word they read. Thousands of left-wingers who listen to the talk show host's statements agree with every word they heard.

Thousands more readers and listeners, of course, are of the strong opinion that they haven't heard or read such a load of yak squeeze in years.

And so it goes—agreement and disagreement, fans and detrac-

[35]Sorry, Stephanie Miller. You haven't sent me any tickets to your "Sexy Liberal Comedy Tour," so I can't judge whether you're funny or not. I have heard some of your statements in support of Obama—and they're certainly funny enough.

tors.

But what happens next?

The columnist retreats into his office, sits down in his leather recliner, pulls out a Cuban, and has a few nice puffs. Those who disagree are more likely to criticize than are those who agree are to praise, so his email in-box fills up with expressions of outrage over his column.

Readers are sending him letters, with copies of articles relating statistics that prove convincingly that the columnist's position on the gun control matter is startlingly wrong. The reality, though, is that he never reads the emails, nor does he see the letters.

The dissenting comments are all carefully screened by some intern or assistant, who is careful to feed his boss' ego with reader accolades, rather than criticism. If one discouraging word should get through, the columnist can choose to either consider or ignore it.

No matter what course he chooses, nobody else is the wiser—especially not the readers. Lately, some newspapers have allowed Internet users to post comments online after these columns. As you might expect, the columnists absolutely *hate* this! Feedback for their eyes only is one thing, but feedback that others can read?

Why, that's just embarrassing!

Contrast the easy and protected professional life of the columnist to that of the liberal talk show host. The liberal talk jock expresses the same views as the writer, perhaps in the very same words, making the same case expertly (well, to a liberal, anyway) and convincingly. Thousands of listeners agree; thousands don't. So far, the scenario plays out pretty much the same, either way.

But wait… what's that sound? *Oh no! It's the telephones!*

While the liberal columnist is enjoying his cigar, the liberal talk show host has to defend his position to a steady stream of callers. The columnist can choose to merely bask in brilliance of his own reflection in the mirror behind his desk, while the talk show host has to spend the next few hours defending his position against arguments based on fact, reason, and logic from callers.

The columnist's isolation allows him to protect his image as a learned man possessed of brilliant ideas. He faces a challenge only if he chooses to do so. The leftist talk show host crumbles under the onslaught of contrarian arguments, and limps to the end of the show humiliated and bowed under the weight of fact and logic. Eventually, this takes a toll on our poor proggie talker. With his credibility destroyed, the ratings plummet and the lib talker finds other work—perhaps as one of the thousands of "Democrat strategists" we see populating cable television news shows.

It would all be so much easier for the liberal talk show hosts if they just didn't have to take phone calls. Then again, after they wrapped up their "America is bad, the United Nations is good; individualism is bad, collectivism is good; capitalism is bad, a government-controlled economy is good; private medical care is bad, socialized medicine is good; private sector spending is bad, government spending is what made America great; Fox News is bad, CBS and CNN are infallible; Obama is "sort of" a god; minorities are bad, and the jury is out on most white people" routine, they might find it hard to fill the remaining two hours and 45 minutes of their show.

Let me make it easier for you to grasp this (though I know you already get it). Here's this simple, basic, easy-to-understand scenario I love to present to liberals, just to see if they can successfully defend a basic tenet of liberalism—government-enforced charity.

I've gone through this routine countless times on the air with liberal callers, and not one of them—not one—has ever successfully withstood the challenge.

I'll be the compassionate, caring and loving liberal for this scenario, and you can be the selfish, stingy, greedy conservative. As we walk along a downtown street, discussing the efficacy of a degree in gender studies in an increasing technological society, we encounter a panhandler.

This poor guy doesn't have any arms or legs, yet he's playing 26 musical instruments, simultaneously. There's a bucket in front of him with a few dollars in it. Behind the bucket is a sign reading, *"Tips please. Thank you. Stump the Band."*

Being the compassionate liberal, I pull out a 5 and put it in Stump's bucket. Then I turn to you and tell you to put $5 in the bucket, too. You say that you just don't have the money to spare. There are bills to pay and mouths to feed.

OK, here's the question: At that point, would it be OK if I were to pull a gun out of my pocket, put that gun to your head and tell you that you don't have a choice? Can I simply use deadly force to make you put a 5-dollar bill in that bucket? I doubt that you're going to say, "Sure! Go ahead. I don't mind!"

Your likely answer here is that I have no right to force you to give.

As I said, I've never had a liberal tell me that it would be OK for me to pull a gun out of my pocket and force them to give to the panhandler. Yet, this is what they do, using the police power of government to seize and transfer (or redistribute, to use Obama's favorite word) wealth, day after day.

OK, fine. Here's my follow-up question: If government derives its power from the consent of the governed, and if I, part of the governed, can't use deadly force to make you give money to someone else, how then can I ask the government to do that for me?

Crickets.

So, what's a good liberal to do?

About what? About talk radio? About the fact that pretty much the only way libs can get a left-leaning talk show lineup on the radio is to buy the time?

Say what? *Buy the time?* Oh, you didn't know about that?

Well, you've no doubt heard of Air America, the great failed experiment in liberal talk radio. Al Franken and Gang?

Yup! *That's the one.*

Actually, it turned out to be the Great Experiment in Broadcast Bankruptcy. A quick look at the history of Air America illustrates why lefty talk on the radio is, with just a few exceptions, pretty much a nonstarter.

First, let's lay out one fundamental difference between what was the Air America crew and syndicated conservative hosts such as

Rush Limbaugh, Sean Hannity, Mike Levin, and the rest, including myself: Air America paid (or had to pay) many of its radio stations to carry their programming.

I am not aware of one major daily syndicated conservative or Libertarian talk show that has had to pay to have its shows aired. The radio stations pay *them*. A combination of very poor ratings and this pay-as-you-go business model—sometimes adding up to hundreds of thousands of dollars a year—is bound to lead to problems.

Problems like, oh, *insolvency*.

There's another way you can make a success out of a liberal radio talk show: Find a liberal who's actually entertaining!

Sure, there are some, though your chances of finding Faith Hill folding towels in an East Los Angeles Laundromat are much better. For liberals with entertainment value, Stephanie Miller comes to mind. Stephanie, though, is a stand-up comic—and beautiful to boot. Does her show draw Hannity-type numbers? No, but she's in there surviving.

It may seem that I revel in the failure of left-wing talk radio. Not so. Oh sure, I get the big chuckle out of some liberal icon like Mario Cuomo proudly announcing his entry into the talk radio wars and falling flat on both of his faces almost immediately.

I also had to laugh when I found out that the founders of Air America actually felt it necessary to embezzle money from a Boy's Club to keep their project afloat. The truth is, though, that I wanted and still want liberals to succeed at talk radio. I believe that there is value in all points of view being floated, so that we can see which ones fly.[36]

When Air America had a fund drive, seeking money to keep the network on the air, I was actually a contributor! Not a George-Soros-type contributor, but a contributor, nonetheless. I even have

---

[36]You will read later that it was I who talked George Bush's State Department into including a liberal talk show host, Stephanie Miller, in a little junket to Europe to talk about the presidential election in London and Dublin.

my Air America tote bag they gave me as thanks.

I'm very careful where I carry this historic relic.

Oh, by the way, I'd like to add just a word or two about the latest liberal methodology in their attempt to destroy talk radio.

It's not talk radio, according to them now—it's "hate" radio.

It seems that whenever you express a negative opinion or disagreement about someone or some idea these days, you are "hating." This means that talk radio is "hate radio."

This mindless, plebian effort at dealing with ideological opponents is not surprising from the left, who use anything to avoid having to deal with uncomfortable ideas using fact or logic.

Just call it "hate." There, now that settles it, right?

Since our proggie friends—well, most of them anyway—are so miserably inept and unsuccessful at this talk radio business, their mindset is such that they simply must find a way to destroy it. To the liberal—especially the big-government variety of this strange species—that which cannot be controlled must be destroyed.

So now you can go back and read about those community advisory boards and the Fairness Doctrine, again.

SECTION II

FUN AND OUTRAGE BEHIND THE MIC

OK, so I've concentrated on the business of talk radio and my four decades as a host. Now it's time to get to some of the wonderful moments I've had on the air. We go from throwing cats out of airplanes to killer dolphins, from infuriating folks after Hurricane Katrina to infuriating them all that much more after the shootings at Virginia Tech. Some of these things didn't occur on the air—they happened to me in real life. Still, my listeners loved the stories and asked that they be repeated often, so I'm including them here.

It's time for some fun and outrage.

CATS, DOGS AND ASSORTED ANIMALS

I love most animals. How much?

Well, let's start with hunters. What the hell is wrong with you people? *Seriously*!

You're out in the wilderness with a bunch of good friends. You wake up to the smell of someone cooking some campfire coffee and frying some bacon. You sit back with a cool breeze rustling through the trees and an early morning mist over the river—and you just can't wait to grab your rifle and head out to find the most perfect deer specimen in the woods, just so you can kill it.

Wow! What a way to enjoy your day!

Or maybe you're a macho big-game hunter! You travel to some thousand-acre ranch in Texas, where a landowner has fenced in exotic animals imported from Africa. He puts you in his ATV and drives you out to an isolated corner of his ranch, where he knows some antelopes are grazing. He points out a small herd and you grab your rifle, find the best animal—and shoot it through the heart!

What a complete stud you are! Ramar of the Jungle!

How does that feel? Does your penis suddenly grow by several inches as soon as you shoot an animal? Does this kick off some glandular response that suddenly heightens your testosterone level by a factor of three or more? Do you feel like you could get all of your alma mater's cheerleaders shouting, "Don't stop! Don't stop!" in unison?

If not, why the hell do you do it?

Back in the 1960s, when I was writing speeches for the governor of Georgia, he became involved in an interesting case involving a black man—a father of three—who lived just south of Atlanta.

The man's family came to visit the governor on one of his periodic "Little People's Day" in the governor's office. On those days, anybody—absolutely anybody—could get into a line winding into the governor's office. Remember? That's how I got my job there in the first place.

When you got to the front of the line, you had the opportunity to ask the governor anything you wished. Most of the people in line were there to ask the governor to get a wrongfully convicted (of course) relative out of a Georgia prison.

This particular man? He had been arrested for shooting a deer out of season.

Why did he commit such a heinous crime? Because his family was hungry, that's why. The man had lost his job and his family was hungry, so he did what man has been doing for thousands of years: He went hunting, and brought home some meat.

Civilization, though, had advanced (if that's the word) to the point that a man could no longer feed his family in this manner—not unless, that is, the government said it was OK. There were certain times of the year, however, when you could kill an animal just for the pure hell of it.

Yes, Governor Maddox interceded and charges against this man were dropped.

I can hear the screams of protest now. Some of you avid hunters won't even read any further in this book. Your loss.

You're saying, "Look, Boortz, if it wasn't for us hunters, there would be (insert animal here) starving out there."

Yeah, right.

So you're telling me that if you're walking through the woods and suddenly see two deer, and one of them is an emaciated, diseased, mangy-looking reject from a third-world petting farm, and the other is healthy and proud with a rack that would make Dolly Parton jealous, you're going to shoot the sick one, right? Yeah, OK. You're going to shoot the sick one, because that's what's best for the herd.

Now, if you can't honestly say, "That's right, Boortz, I would shoot the sick one," then don't give me this Bolshoi about deer hunters as conservationists.

We both know the truth ain't in ya.

And you bow hunters? JC and the disciples! Can you imagine what it feels like to suddenly have an arrow piercing your chest? Doesn't matter, though. Just as long as you feel like a man and your buddies are impressed, that's what counts.

Actually, I admit that I may be a little extreme here. I don't even like to see animals hunting animals. I know it happens, but that doesn't mean I have to watch it.

A few years ago, National Geographic had a TV series named "Planet Earth." I was really looking forward to watching this, but never made it through the first episode.

It seemed that the director of this effort felt the most important thing he could possibly show the viewers in this TV series is how animals chase down, kill and then eat other animals. You couldn't watch for more than three minutes without being treated to some animal ripping the throat out of another.

I wish that National Geographic had produced another version for obsessive compulsives such as myself—one that showed the scenery and the animals in all their wonder, without all the killing and chowing down.

OK, let's get to dogs.

I'm a committed dog person.

Dogs, I believe, are supernatural beings. At least, some of them are. I know my proud beast Coco definitely fit into that category.

In the spring of 1992, I piloted an Angel Flight from Atlanta to St. Louis. Angel Flight is an organization where member pilots use their own airplanes to fly critically ill patients who cannot afford air travel, or people with needs the airlines simply can't meet, to receive needed medical care.

I returned to Atlanta from St. Louis and managed to crawl into bed just before midnight. I leaned over to get a welcoming smooch from Donna, but instead got a tongue up my nose.

Nope, not a people tongue, but a little, itty-bitty critter tongue.

I let out a yell and Donna turned on the light. There, curled up next to her on the pillow, was a 10-ounce dog she had "found" at a pet store in the mall just hours before.

"It's a Papillion," she said, "and its name is Coco."

"It's a little girl?"

"No, it's a boy."

"A boy named Coco?"

"He's named after my favorite dog I had when I was a kid."

So Coco it was. I know a guy whose dad is named Shirley, so figured I could survive this name. At this point in our marriage, I had figured out where to start arguments, and where to shut up.

Now, I've had big dogs all my life: a Boxer when I was growing up, an ill-tempered Schnauzer, plus a Malamute and about 16 Golden Retrievers (thanks to an incestuous relationship between my stud Rocky and that bitch sister of his).

Big dogs are just fine, but I'm telling you now that nothing beats a smaller dog—a Papillion—for ease of management (you don't really own a dog, despite what you may think) and companionship.

By the time Coco had grown to maturity, he had developed several interesting habits. One was that, when he peed, he would always stand on his front paws, hike his rear end straight up in the air, and walk along leaving a scent trail behind him.

A doggie behavioral expert told me that this was Coco trying to appear bigger than his five pounds. We dog lovers know that dogs are marking territory when they pee on fire hydrants, tree trunks, shrubs and Chris Matthew's legs. Well, apparently other dogs will make a determination of the size of the dog whose territory they are invading by just how high the pee goes.

Little Coco was inflating his size by getting that stream up there as high as he could. Now what cat would think of that?

Coco's other nasty little habit was his bear. Coco had a rather plain-looking little Teddy bear. This bear was Coco's Judy doll. I'm tellin' you, Coco would absolutely wear this little bear out.

Just in case there are some of you who are not really sure what I'm describing, let me elaborate. When Coco was feeling a little randy, he would go get that bear, turn it around so that it was positioned perfectly, hold the bear to him with his front paws, and proceed to make that bear write bad checks.

We had to replace these bears quite often and always had a few new ones in reserve.

Coco was so proud of his little trick that he just had to show it off to anyone who visited. The routine was always the same: Coco would bark, sniff and welcome everyone to our home, and then disappear. Donna and I would exchange knowing glances and, sure enough, within moments, Coco would be back with the bear—the Gummy Bear, as it came to be known.

He would get out there right in the middle of the floor and proceed to—please pardon the expression—screw the stuffing out of that thing. Reactions ranged from shock to amusement.

One particular U.S. Senator, who shall forever remain unnamed, wanted to take him to DC to see if he would do that at a committee meeting. We weren't about to allow Coco to be corrupted by Washington. They do that to taxpayers in Washington. Coco just did it to an inanimate stuffed bear. Maybe if we got stuffed bears for politicians, things would calm down a bit.

Coco was in his finest form when I took him to the radio station to spend the morning with me doing the show. The bear would come, too, of course.

By total coincidence, Coco would just happen to visit the *WSB* studios on the very same days—Tuesdays and Thursdays—that tours were coming through. Truth be told, I had a rather contentious relationship with some of the tour guides—especially one particular guide who was the quintessential Southern prude.

It was my fault, really. One tour day, years before, I had taken the pages out of an "I Hate Cats" calendar and posted them in the studio window for the kids in the tour to see. Let's see, there were pictures of kittens in boil-n-bags being held over a pot of boiling water, and of a cat wrapped in aluminum foil on the barbecue. Then there was the cat buried up to its neck in a lawn surrounded by horseshoes. The tour guides complained, I took the pictures down, and war was declared.

So here's how it would work with my proud beast: The tour guides would usher a bunch of wide-eyed kids to the window in my studio. I would then take the bear and toss it on the table between the kids and me.

As I shouted, "Coco! Get your bear," Royal, seeing what was coming, would start playing "Who Let the Dogs Out" on the air and Coco would leap into action. Those kids would get a lesson they didn't expect while visiting the studios of *The Neal Boortz Show*.

Soon, the managers issued a general prohibition on bringing dogs into the station. If you think that slowed me down one bit, you haven't been reading this book with the proper degree of attention.

Coco's last two years were pretty rough. He lost his hearing. That was my fault, I suppose. I would fly him back and forth from Atlanta to our home in Naples, without him having any hearing protection. Now they have mutt-muffs for flying dogs. Coco wasn't that lucky.

Then he lost an eye when attacked by another dog. Soon, he was essentially blind. At about 17 years old, on the very day that Donna was heading to the West Coast with friends, Coco had a stroke.

As Donna left that morning, I told her that I would take Coco to the vet and do everything I could to keep him alive until she got back. I left my little buddy with the vet and went to the studios.

Later that morning, our vet called me and said it was time—Coco was suffering. I told him to go ahead. That afternoon, my friend Ray Goff, a former Georgia Bulldog head coach, sat with me at the Starbucks at Atlanta's Lenox Square and we talked about dogs—for hours.

That night, the folks at *WSB* took me to the St. Regis Bar in Atlanta—and then it was up to Belinda to see that I got home without driving. To this day, I feel terrible guilt that I wasn't there for Coco—wasn't holding him and stroking him—when he breathed his last.

As I type these words, though, Coco is about eight inches to the right of the keyboard in his brass urn. He's there—I can feel his presence—and, sometimes, I can see him sitting across the room watching me work.

There will never be another dog like him.

Truly my second best friend.

THE WHITE PERSIAN CAT FROM HELL

Let's be real: There is no possible way you can ever become as attached to a cat as you can a dog.

Dogs love you. Cats tolerate you.

No one disputes that.

When a cat nuzzles you, it is not showing affection. It is leaving its scent. And, if you have a cat in the house, the *last* thing you want to do is shine a black light into a darkened room along baseboards, drapes and furniture bottoms. The telltale signs of your lovely cat's territory-marking escapades would jump out at you in glorious phosphorescent living color.

The cat would be gone the next day.

Besides, they drop deuces in your potted plants.

When we were first married, we had this white Persian named

MAYBE I SHOULD JUST SHUT UP AND GO AWAY! | 133

Chi Chi of Kalakawa. The name is from the street where the Outrigger Hotel, our honeymoon hotel, is located in Waikiki.

This cat had only one endearing quality: She would chase those little wire cages that you take off the top of champagne bottles—fetch them, if you will—and bring them back to you.

Wonderful.

This cat's only good quality was that it sometimes acted like a dog.

Swell.

Donna and I bought our first home in 1974, and the cat moved in with us. Do you remember your pride in your first home? Same with us. To us, that home was a castle—a 1,250-square-foot castle.

About a year after we moved in, Chi Chi started showing up walking around the house and jumping up on the bed with black feet. Black grimy feet.

Snow-white cat, black feet and grimy black paw prints everywhere the cat went. Get the picture?

We would clean the cat and, a few hours later, she would be back, tracking black grime. Now, mind you, this was an indoor cat. Whatever was happening was happening indoors.

The next Saturday morning, the mystery was solved. We were having a party that night, and I was in the living room getting things ready. Suddenly, the cat went tearing into the fireplace. I went over to swat the cat and noticed a fine layer of soot—that would be BLACK soot.

As I leaned over to pick up the cat, I heard a noise. Something was thrashing around in the chimney. As the thrashing and banging continued, a fine layer of soot worked its way past the damper and settled into the fireplace. Chi Chi came out of the fireplace and started leaving those black, sooty footprints around the house.

OK, here's where things got interesting. Try to keep up.

Something was in the chimney. The party was hours away. I had to get the mystery straightened out.

So I got down on my hands and knees and reached for the damper handle.

First stupid move.

I opened the damper and *hello*. There was a bird in the chimney, and that bird had been banging around there for about two days, knocking every bit of soot off the walls of chimney. All of that soot was sitting on the damper, waiting for some idiot to pull the handle.

I was that idiot.

Down came the soot and, with it, the bird. At that point, I had a fireplace with a pile of soot and a flapping bird—and here comes the damned cat.

Cat jumps into soot after bird. Bird flies into living room. Cat follows bird.

BLACK cat, I should say, follows bird... over the couch... behind the couch... across the carpet... on top of the TV... *you get the picture.*

Those two conducted a most thorough tour of the entire living and dining rooms. Finally, the cat caught the bird, I caught the cat, grabbed the bird and threw it out the door. The cat got locked in the bathroom while I surveyed the damage.

Everything—and I mean everything—was covered with soot. I tried the vacuum, but that just wasn't going to get the job done. So, while Donna cleaned the cat (resisting the urge to strangle it), I vacuumed as thoroughly as possible and then headed to the local grocery store to rent a carpet cleaner.

By the time I finished cleaning the carpet and furniture, we were about four hours away from party time.

Four hours—and a damp carpet and furniture. How to get it dry? Well I, being so smart and all, had an idea. We could draw air across it, in hopes that it would be reasonably dry by the time the guests arrived.

So how do you draw air across the carpeting and furniture? You mean you don't know? Simple! You simply turn on the 500-horsepower, whole-house attic fan you had installed only months before! That sucker could set up a breeze through the house that would blow pictures off the walls.

My brilliant plan was to put the attic fan to work, while I returned the carpet cleaner.

I trotted upstairs (not, by the way, using the T-Rex pose Obama likes to use going up the steps of Air Force One) and hit the switch for the attic fan. The grill flapped open as the big blades start to pick up speed.

"Turn it off! Turn it off! Turn that damned thing off! Oh my God!"

The shriek was from Donna, downstairs trying to straighten some things out. I ran downstairs to see a living room enveloped in a black fog. Yes, thank you very much, that attic fan would draw quite a lot of air across the living room. But, if the chimney is the only thing you have open, all of that air is going to come through the chimney—and through the chimney it came at about force-4, carrying every bit of remaining soot with it.

As Donna and I sat and surveyed the scene in horror, black soot settled on every surface in the living room—every *wet* surface in the living room.

What then? New carpets and new furniture, that's what then. Oh, and the party? We moved it to the condo clubhouse and regaled our guests with the story of that afternoon.

Chi Chi of Kalakawa?

Let's just say we had a cat person working at the station who took immediate custody. It was either that or animal control.

CHASING CATS

It's sad to think that a 42-year talk radio career could result in only one indelible memory in the minds of so many, but I fear that is indeed the case for a lot of my long-term listeners.

That memory was of The Georgia Cat Chasing Championship.

At a meeting of the Georgia Balloon Association[37] sometime in the late 1980s, I found a copy of a newsletter from a ballooning group in Albuquerque, New Mexico. There, buried toward the back, was a single paragraph about cat chasing—the game of throwing perfectly good cats out of balloons and then allowing a group of skydivers to jump out and chase the cat down. The person who landed with the cat was the winner.

I really never bothered to check to see whether or not these Albuquerque balloonists were actually doing this—it smelled like nothing more than a good story to me—but the idea for a nice little talk-radio hoax started to form in my demented consciousness.

So it came to pass that I announced an upcoming remote broadcast to my Atlanta *WGST* listening audience:

"Ladies and gentlemen, let me tell you something we're going to be doing here on *The Neal Boortz Show* sometime in the next few weeks. I'm sure you haven't heard of this, but there's a sport out there called cat chasing. Sometime near the end of the year, the national cat-chasing championships are going to be held in Albuquerque, New Mexico. A group of skydivers from Georgia that I've met while ballooning want to send someone to compete in the nationals, so they're going to hold the *Georgia Cat Chasing Championships* in about four weeks. We're going to be there to bring it to you live on the show.

"Now let me tell you how this works: We put about six skydivers and one cat into an airplane and climb up to 14,000 feet. As the plane approaches the target, they throw the cat out of the airplane. All of the skydivers follow immediately and give chase. The skydivers have about 10,000 feet to catch the cat—and the person who lands with the cat is declared the winner. We have about 30 or so skydivers who will be participating, so there will be five jumps and we'll be there to bring it all to you on the show."

That was it. That was all I said on the first day. Figured I would just let the listeners stew over that one for a while. Sooner or later, I knew someone was going to call the show to inquire about the contest and register disgust and displeasure.

---

[37]Before I started flying airplanes, I was an aeronaut. That's the fancy word given to people who fly hot air balloons. I got my first hot air balloon in the mid-1970s and flew these bags of hot air—I know, how ironic—until around 1990. Truth is, they're somewhat safer, but a good deal more difficult to fly than single-engine airplanes.

As it turned out, it was sooner rather than later.

Almost immediately, the calls of protest started to come in. People were concerned about the safety of the cats used in this competition. Hard to explain, I know, but there were actually some people out there who were upset over the possibility that the cat might be injured. At this point, I knew I had something good going on—something I could milk for attention and controversy for quite a few weeks.

"What if nobody catches the cat?"

"Well, that seldom happens, but we're pretty sure that the cat would be OK."

"How can you say that? You're throwing that cat out over two miles in the air."

"Yeah, well that's just the point! The farther the cat has to fall, the better the cat's chance of survival! That's why we don't start the jump any closer to the ground!"

"No cat can survive a free fall from 14,000 feet!"

"Sure they can. Haven't you heard of the zone of death for cat falls?"

"What zone of death?"

"Well, this happened in New York City. The animal-welfare folks in New York started to see some interesting statistics on cats falling out of skyscrapers. If the cats fell from one of the first few floors, they might die but, if they fell from above the sixth floor, they usually survived."

"Oh yeah, sure."

"No, really! You see, if you give these cats enough time to stabilize themselves as they fall, they actually get all splayed out—sorta like a flying squirrel—and, when they land, they kinda bounce. Really, look it up. Besides, they're only cats."

Look it up? Yeah, sure. Remember, this was before the Internet. There is no way you could get away with something like this today. Some listener would be Googling "cat chase" and mess up my fun in a real hurry. As it turns out, this bit about cats surviving falls above a certain height turns out to be absolutely true. Really—look it up. Google "Terminal velocity of cats" and see what you find.

The hoax took form over the ensuing weeks as I kept promoting our live coverage of *The Georgia Cat Chasing Championships* "from some airport in South Georgia." The "some airport" part was necessary, I explained, because some animal welfare do-gooders were trying to figure out where this little event was going to take place, so that they could take steps to stop it.

"These cats must be protected!"

At one point, I brought about five sky-diving buddies into the studio to pose as experienced cat chasers. With only the briefest explanation of what we were trying to pull off here, these guys were on their game. One of them, faking an Australian accent as the Aussie cat-chasing champ, even sang us the Australian cat-chasing song:

"Well, it's heave-ho! Out you go!"

These guys supplied the story of the only known human fatality from cat chasing. Once a skydiver caught the cat, you see, they didn't have to worry about holding on to him. They would simply press the cat up against their jumpsuit and the cat, having had quite enough of the free-fall thing at that point, would latch on with its claws until the skydiver landed. At that point, the cat would usually run like hell—never to be seen again.

Well, they had been strays when we found them, anyway, so no problem, right?

But, on one fateful occasion, a cat managed to attach itself to the parachute pack, instead of the front of the contestant's jump suit. The unfortunately positioned cat prevented the deployment of the chute when the ripcord was pulled. Tragically, neither the cat nor the jumper survived that one.

Today, you can see the cat—stuffed, of course—still attached to the parachute pack in a biker bar just outside of Clovis, New Mexico.

When we were about one week away from the alleged remote broadcast of the *Georgia Cat Chasing Championships*, we were getting no small amount of attention. I was being threatened with lawsuits.

"How could I be sued for this?" I asked. "I'm not the one throwing cats out of airplanes. I'm just covering this event. I'm reporting. I can't be held responsible for an event that I'm merely reporting on."

The frustration among irate listeners increased. There didn't seem to be any way they could stop this travesty from happening.

Now it was time to get ready for the show—the remote broadcast. We started gathering together the sound effects we would need: Wind noise, airplane noise, calm cats, howling cats, helicopters, crowd noise, screaming, applause, parachutes popping open, chain saws, sirens, cheers, bands—you name it. Oh, and we needed the sound of a cat hitting the ground at terminal velocity. That would be about 120 miles per hour.[38]

Actually, the broadcast almost didn't happen. As I got out of my car that morning in the station parking lot, I was approached by the county sheriff. Not a deputy, mind you—this was the actual man himself.

He demanded that I tell him where this event was going to take place. I told him I wouldn't. He then told me that he was getting phone calls from all over South Georgia, from various county sheriffs who had been advised by crazed cat lovers that this event was going to take place in their county.

In fact, he told me, several South Georgia airports were under surveillance by local law enforcement. I told him to wait outside and he could follow me when I left the station. Of course, I didn't tell him that I would be leaving the station after the show—and after the *fake* broadcast. (When I did finally leave, he was nowhere in sight.)

So, on with the broadcast. Cue the crowd! Cue the marching bands! Cue the airplanes taking off! Cue the wind noise as we

---

[38]We discovered that the sound of a terminal-velocity cat could be most closely approximated by dropping an entire cow's liver on a microphone from the top of a stepladder. Hey, we were a big-budget operation here. No cutting corners.

opened the airplane door to throw the cats out! Cue the screaming cats! Cue the chain saw!

Chain saw?

Well, you see, one of the cats actually eluded capture by one of the jumpers and landed in a pine tree. We had to use the chain saw to cut down the pine tree to get the cat down.[39] The tree hit the ground. Cue the falling tree! The cat hit the trail and hasn't been seen since.

The great *Georgia Cat Chasing Championship* went on for an hour, with excellent commentary from my skydiving buddies, when suddenly I realized I had about 20 seconds to close this thing out.

About all I could say was "This was all faked, folks. Stay tuned for the news" and we were out of there.

I walked out of the studio to what I fully expected would be the shouts of approval from station staff. Didn't turn out that way.

Instead, I faced a wall of irate sales weasels. It seems most of our advertisers were getting hammered by listeners upset with our apparent cat-abuse game. At least one advertiser, Home Depot, had called and cancelled its entire advertising contract.

Oh well, that's just the stuff you have to put up with when you're selling advertising for a talk radio show. Those weasels all make six figures (even then), so it's a small price to pay.

Mind you, they weren't the only ones upset. Animal-rights activists across the country heard about the show, even though I was just an insignificant local talk show host at the time.[40]

---

[39]Cats out of trees. This reminds me of an interesting ballooning tale. Much ado in the neighborhood one afternoon with a cat caught in a tree. The local fire department was in no mood to be bothered, so a bright idea was formed. There were virtually no winds, so I would get some neighborhood help and fetch the cat with my hot air balloon. So, we spread the balloon out and inflated it. About 45 seconds of blasting from the heater brought it upright, and we attached tether lines. I then gently gained altitude to cat level as the ground crew brought me closer to the tree.

Do you have any idea what a cat will do at the approach of a 55,000-cubic-foot balloon with a 15-million BTU heater that sounds like a dragon? No? Well, you don't WANT to know.

[40]It would be about 10 years before I would become an insignificant nationally syndicated talk show host.

Since the show was getting so much attention, we took the tape and had it reproduced on cassettes. We then sold copies of the cat chase for 10 bucks—with proceeds going to an animal-protection group.

We sold hundreds of tapes and raised thousands for the poor little animals. I stipulated that the money be used to save dogs and puppies. Maybe bunnies.

No cats.

KILLER DOLPHINS

Most of you probably won't remember, but there was a little bit of a controversy going on back in early 1977 in California.

It seems that California tuna fishermen were catching Flipper's relatives in their nets. Super-sensitive California New-Age bell-bottom-jeans-wearing types tend to get their bikinis in a knot when dolphins die in tuna nets.

This controversy formed the basis for another fun spoof.

How in the world did I take a news story about dolphins and tuna boats in California and turn it into more than three days of fun on the radio? To tell you the truth, I'm not exactly sure myself. I'm guessing *National Lampoon* magazine came up with the idea.

Here's how it played out:

I was in law school at the time, handling the radio show in the afternoons. One of my classmates, Harvey, was quite bright, and somewhat of a cut up, so he would be a perfect accomplice.

So—for the purposes of my radio show, at least—Harvey became a renowned oceanographer from Southern California.

It was Wednesday, March 30, 1977.

At some point during the show on that day, I introduced my guest.

"Ladies and gentlemen, as you know, there has been a great deal of controversy in California over dolphins and tuna fishermen. People are upset that tuna fishermen are catching dolphins in their nets, and dolphins are dying.

"Well, knowing how much y'all like dolphins, I have the opportunity to bring you a special guest," I continued. "On the phone, the director of the San Diego Marine Research Institute, Dr. Harvey Seagal."

Harvey, in case you haven't figured this out yet, was in the next room on the phone. The conversation between Dr. Seagal and myself was actually pretty dull. In other words, it was a typical guest interview.

As we came out of the first commercial break, I baited the trap.

"Our guest today is Dr. Harvey Seagal, of the San Diego..."

"Uh, excuse me. Mr., ahhhh, Boortz, is it?"

"Yes, Dr. Rhymes with sports."

"Well, Mr. Boortz. I'm terribly sorry, but we have a bit of an emergency here at the Institute that I need to deal with, so I'm going to have to end the interview. I'm very sorry."

Click.

That was it. He was gone. Hung up.

So I offered my apologies to the audience and we just went on talking about something else. What? I have no idea. Maybe Vietnam. Who knows? It's not like I was keeping logs or anything like that.

Then came the very next day, Thursday, March 31.

This time, I came to the studios with not only Harvey, but also two other law school friends in tow. They sat in the adjoining room with their telephones while I began the show.

I began with a completely innocuous topic. Perhaps it was the perfectly hideous job Jimmy Carter was doing in the White House. About 40 minutes into the show (I didn't want to appear too anxious), the first call came through from one of my friends in the next room—a lady.

"Sandy. You're on the air."

"Hi, Mr. Boortz. Long time listener, first time caller, but I just had to tell you something odd."

"What's that?"

"Well, I have a son in the Coast Guard, you see, and he just called me from his base on Coronado Island in San Diego."

"And said what?"

"Well, he told me that they—the Coast Guard—that they were having some trouble with dolphins in the San Diego Area. He says—and I know this sounds ridiculous, but he's my son and I believe him—he says that dolphins are jumping onto tuna boats and killing the crews."

"Yeah, sure. With what? Guns? Nice try Sandy, but I gotta move on here."

"No, wait! I'm telling you the truth!"

"Yeah, yeah, yeah. Nice try. Thanks for the call, Sandy."

I immediately put another call on the air, and we resumed normal conversation, apparently forgetting Sandy's call.

About 15 minutes later, it was time for law school friend No. 2 to make his call:

"Tony, you're on the air."

"Neal, listen. Don't hang up. *Listen.* Remember that lady who called about her son in the Coast Guard in San Diego?"

"Yeah, but wha..."

"No, wait! Remember yesterday? You were talking to that doctor or something from San Diego? Dr., ahhhh..."

"Siegal. Harvey Seagal."

"Yeah! That's him! Well, don't you remember that he told you he had an emergency, and he had to go, and then he hung up the phone? And now that lady calls..."

"Tony, you're absolutely right. That does seem to be a rather odd coincidence. Tell you what, we have a commercial break coming up, and I'm going to find Dr. Seagal's phone number. I have it here in yesterday's notes and will call him when we get back. Thanks for the tip!"

Commercial break.

When we came back, I was making another call to my friend Harvey, who was in the next room.

"Hello?"

"Dr. Seagal?"

"Yes. Who is this?"

"It's Neal Boortz, Dr. Sie..."

"How did you get this phone number?"

"You were a guest on my show yesterday, remember? You suddenly hung up..."

"Yeah well, I really can't talk to you right now. You see, we have this little problem..."

"Is it about those dolphins, Dr. Seagal? The dolphins that are killing fishermen?"

"How did you find about that? Nobody knows about that!"

"Well, some lady with a son in the Coast Guard called, and we just put two and two together and decided to call you.

There was a long pause. Finally, a sigh.

"Dr. Seagal?"

"OK. I guess the story is going to get out sooner or later, so let me tell you what's happening, so you won't just be dealing with rumors.

"You see, here at the San Diego Marine Research Institute, we have a classified program where we're training dolphins for warfare. These dolphins—they're very smart, you know—are taught reconnaissance, how to disarm basic underwater explosive devices, how to handle simple and not-so simple weapons systems, and a lot more."

"Yes sir?"

"Well, about a week or so ago, about three of these dolphins escaped their pen on Coronado Island. Now it looks like they've rounded up some other dolphins and they're attacking tuna boats and killing the tuna fishermen. The fishermen seem to think it's in retaliation for so many dolphins being caught in their nets."

"Killing fishermen? How would they kill fishermen?"

"Well, they're trained warfare dolphins, you understand, so they jump into the boats and just fin the fishermen to death."

"How many fishermen have they killed?"

"We're not sure. We've found about six, but there are several tuna boats missing."

"How do you know it was dolphins?"

"We have a witness."

"What do you mean, a witness? Somebody saw this happen?"

"Well, one fisherman—the only one in his crew that survived—shimmied up the mast of the tuna boat. Dolphins, you may know, can't shimmy, so they just crashed this boat onto some rocks and swam away. That's where we found him. Crashed on the rocks near La Jolla. He told us the story."

We went on to talk to "Dr. Seagal" for the better part of the next half hour. He told us that he was certain his trained warfare dolphins were behind this, because the surviving tuna fisherman spotted the special harness they wear. He also gave us an idea of these dolphins' capabilities. They could, for instance, operate vessels and knew how to communicate through Morse code.

We hung up with Dr. Seagal, but weren't through setting the hook.

Remember that this was 1977. There were basically three television networks, and that was pretty much it for instantaneous news coverage. You couldn't just go to the Internet or to Google and search for killer dolphins and wrecked tuna boats.

This was allegedly happening on the other side of the country. The fact that this story hadn't made it to the evening TV news or the papers yet meant nothing. We were really treating it as our own breaking story.

We made one final call before the show was over on Thursday, March 31. This time we made the call—and the person who answered, once again, was in the other room.

"Oceanside Coast Guard."

"Hello! My name is Neal Boortz, and I'm a talk show host in Atlanta."

"What can I do for you?"

"Well, I've been talking to some people about some problems you're having with trained warfare dolphins and..."

"Who told you about that?"

"I'm sorry, but I can't tell you. Can I ask you some questions?"

"We have no comment."

Click.

There. The hook was firmly set, and we were at the end of the show. The five of us gathered at a local watering hole to celebrate our good times and future law careers. Clearly, we were going to be fantastic lawyers.

And then came Friday, April 1, 1977.

Did you notice the date? Yup, April Fools Day. But we weren't through with the listeners, yet. On this day, I only needed Harvey. Since some callers might have put some dates together, we had to spring the grand climax as soon as I went on the air.

Harvey was waiting on the phone.

"Ladies and gentlemen, I have some rather serious news for you this morning. We don't really want to ruin your weekend, and after all, this is happening on the West Coast. But if you've been following the show the last few days, you will know that we have a rather serious situation in California relating to the escape of some of the Navy's trained warfare dolphins and the deaths of perhaps a dozen or more tuna fishermen. Now just before I went on the air, I received a phone call from Dr. Harvey Seagal, the marine researcher who has been talking to us about this situation.

"Dr. Seagal, good afternoon."

"Not really, Neal. I'm afraid we have a bit of a crisis situation here, and I can't seem to be able to get the local authorities to believe me on this one."

"What's happening?"

"Well, you'll remember that I told you these dolphins that escaped were trained in military warfare tactics?"

"Yes sir, I remember."

"And that they were capable of operating smaller and more basic Naval vessels."

"Well, yeah. I don't know if that's exactly what you told us, but go on!"

"Well, evidently they're trained far better than we thought—either that or they're capable of learning."

"Why? What happened?"

"Well, Mr. Boortz. The dolphins—*our* dolphins, I think—have seized control of one of our nuclear submarines."

"Aw, come on Dr. Seagal. You've *got* to be kidding me."

"I only wish I was, Mr. Boortz. But they now have control of a nuclear submarine."

"OK... so how are these dolphins going to get control of a nuke sub?"

"They swam up the torpedo tubes. They swam right into the submarine and took over. They're holding some crewmen hostage."

"Yeah, sure."

"No! Mr. Boortz! You have to believe me here! You have to tell the authorities that you've been talking to me about this for three days! You were practically there when it happened, when they escaped. The authorities just have to be convinced."

"Why, Dr.? It's not as if they're going to run off with the submarine."

"That's just it! They *have*!" The submarine is just below the surface about 30 miles off the coast of Los Angeles right now! And, Mr. Boortz, the dolphins are making threats."

"Threats? What do you mean making threats? Are they squeaking to you over the radio? Come on, Dr. Get serious here."

"No! Not the radio! I told you! They know Morse code! They're sending us signals in Morse code by beating something against the hull of the submarine!"

"What are they saying?"

"We have to stop the tuna fishermen. They're going to do something horrible if we don't stop the fishermen."

"What could they possibly do? Ram a fishing boat?"

"No, Mr. Boortz. They have nukes."

"They *what*? Just what are you saying, Dr. Seagal?"

"They have nukes. Nuclear missiles. That's a Polaris nuclear submarine they've taken, and they are saying they're going to nuke Los Angeles if we don't scuttle... if we don't sink all of the tuna boats now!"

"Can they do that?"

"They managed to steal a nuclear submarine, didn't they?"

"OK, Dr. Seagal. What's next?"

"You, Mr. Boortz. You're next. You have to call the authorities in California and convince them that this is serious. I know you called the Coast Guard the other day. And there's that lady who has a son serving in the Coast Guard. You gotta get their attention, Mr. Boortz. You gotta!"

Seagal hung up.

Ya know, there is some point where you've played a gag out just about as far as you can. I can imagine listeners with friends and relatives in Los Angles wetting themselves about now—and calling their friends to tell them they're in danger.

So it was time to pay this off and run for cover.

"By the way, folks. Have you looked at the calendar? APRIL FOOLS! Harvey, come in here!"

Harvey entered the studio.

"Here he is, folks. Harvey Seagal, though this time not on a phone. Harvey is a law school buddy of mine and I want you to know that every bit of this was his idea."

"Oh great, now they're probably going to reject me for a license to practice law."

We then spent about a half hour yukking it up amongst ourselves and talking with some callers about how thoroughly we had fooled them.

Now you would think that was the end of this story.

It wasn't.

No, there were no recriminations from the FCC, and the management of the station had no problem with what we had done. People were tuning in, and that's always a good thing.

But at the very moment we were announcing that this was all an April Fool's prank, there was a Delta jet somewhere over the middle of the country on the way to San Diego. On that jet, you would find a reporter and a photographer for the *Atlanta Constitution*.

You see, as I told you, this was before the Internet. Inquiries had been made, of course, and denials heard. But there was that chance—that slim chance—that Boortz over at *WRNG* was really onto something here, so they had better send a reporter out there.

When the reporters got to San Diego, they phoned in—and were told to get back on a plane and come back home.

A week or so later, *WRNG* got a bill from the *Atlanta Constitution* for airfare and a room for two intrepid journalists.

To the best of my knowledge, that bill remains unpaid.

FLYING NEKKID

Certainly you know, if you've been listening to me for any length of time at all, that flying is one of my passions. My dad was a Marine Corps pilot. He flew in World War II, Korea and Vietnam. He never talked much about his wartime flying. That's not unusual for combat pilots, I'm told.

I remember that, when I first learned that my dad could fly airplanes, I was in complete awe. I recall looking at him, then looking at his hands, and thinking "Holy cow! My dad can fly an airplane!"

As far back as I can remember, my favorite toy was anything that could fly. I always had some 25-cent balsa wood gliders around. When I really wanted to splurge, I would take some of my allowance and buy a small airplane with a plastic propeller that wound up with a rubber band. Those marvelous flying machines could set me back as much as a buck 25.

Being a high-performance kind of balsa pilot, I would double up on the rubber bands to see just how far I could get that baby to fly. When I lost or destroyed these toys, there were always exciting new paper airplane designs to explore next.

I took my first flight in a light single-engine airplane when I was a junior at Pensacola High School. The flight school at Pensacola's airport was promoting "penny a pound" airplane rides one weekend, so I got my $1.65 together[41] and rode my bike to the airport. We took about a five-minute ride around the bayou and landed.

At that point, it was inevitable: I was going to learn how to fly. There was just no way around it—I was hooked. I had no idea how I was going to be able to afford it, but it was going to happen.

Fast forward to the early 1970's and DeKalb-Peachtree Airport (PDK) in Atlanta. I was doing my talk show at that time on *WRNG*. A PDK flight school rep cornered a sales weasel with an offer: They wanted me to do a personal endorsement of their flight school. (Even then, I talked incessantly about flying, though I had never taken a lesson.)

In return for my endorsement of their flight school in paid advertisements on the air, they would give me lessons up to and including my first solo flight.

DEAL! I got my plotter, an E6B flight computer, a logbook and showed up for my first lesson.

OK, here's where I made my first mistake. The deal was that they were going to give me lessons until I flew the airplane alone. Nothing was said about ground school. Nothing was said about a minimum number of hours of instruction. Once you solo the airplane, your lessons are over—unless you want to pay for them.

First lesson: I was told to take off in the airplane, then we went out and did some straight and level flying. Believe it or not, the instructor then actually talked me through landing the airplane, a Cessna 152, at the end of my first lesson.

So far so good.

---

[41]It would cost me about $2.25 now. I looked like a refugee in high school. Crew cut. Ribs showing. And dark, horn-rimmed glasses with—I swear—adhesive tape on the bridge.

I wasn't smart enough to know that I was costing the flight school money here, and the sooner I soloed the airplane, the sooner they were off the hook. On my sixth lesson, the instructor had me pull over to the apron after a few landings.

Six lessons! A little less than six hours of flight instruction! And this instructor tells me that I am going to fly the airplane—alone—around the pattern for three takeoffs and landings. Was he kidding? I was going to fly an airplane all by myself![42]

No, there's no amazing story to be told here. I made the three circuits, taxied back to the flight school, and let them cut the tail of my shirt. The instructor then wrote something about my first solo, the tail number of the airplane, and a little drawing of a 152 on that cloth.

I have that shirttail to this day.

Now the truth is—a truth later realized—I was nowhere near ready to solo an airplane after five-and-a-half or six hours. The lessons ended there (for the time being), because I just didn't have the money to continue.

But, by God, I had done it! I had flown an airplane all alone—with nobody there but me to get that sucker back on the ground, without breaking anything or drawing blood.

Even sitting here, typing these words into the computer, I can feel the sheer elation of that moment. It's perhaps even better than your first… um… ahhh… *oh never mind.*

Suffice it to say that most everyone has that first, but not so with flying an airplane. If you've even given the faintest whisper of a thought to taking flying lessons, I cannot urge you enough to go out there and just do it!

---

[42]The flight instructor was really more interesting in building hours for a shot at the airlines than he was in quality instruction. His favorite routine was to pull back the throttle to idle—and an airplane won't fly at idle throttle, by the way—and then say "OK, you just lost your engine. Where you gonna land?" You would start gliding to a spot that looked big enough to put the airplane down. At the last possible second, he would give you your power back and you would climb out to do it all, again. One day, he gave the power back a bit late to another student. They ended up in a tree—with a branch sticking through the instructor's thigh. Goodbye, airline career.

It doesn't matter whether or not you ever actually get your license. Just get that first solo under your belt. When you pull back on the mixture and shut the engine down after that solo flight, you will be filled with a feeling of accomplishment, adrenaline and pride that you may not match for many, many years. *Just do it!*

Anyways…

I don't know the date. Don't even know the year—doesn't matter. I do know it was after I got my pilot's license, but before I ever owned my first airplane.

I had a speech scheduled in Jekyll Island, Georgia. *Fantastic!* This would be my first chance to actually use an airplane for something other than boring holes in the sky and making turns around a point!

The plan was to fly from PDK to Jekyll Island (09J), a distance of 222 nautical miles, the afternoon before the speech. I would have my say, hit the sack, and then get up and fly back to Atlanta. So I headed to the airport, rented a Cherokee 140, and headed SE to Jekyll.

OK. Here's where I learned something they didn't teach me in flight school. This flight was going to take me about two hours. That means you have to have enough fuel in the tanks, and enough unfilled space in your bladder for a flight of that duration.

I was fine on the fuel part, but I had been drinking water like a fish that morning—and the bladder was nagging at me almost as soon as I took off.

"I can hold it," I'm thinking. "I can hold this. No problem."

Problem.

About one hour into the flight, it became clear that there was no way I was going to make it to Jekyll without draining the sumps (so to speak). But flying isn't like driving. You don't just pull into a rest area and let 'er rip.

It takes no less than 40 minutes at best to find an airport, do the approach and landing, shut things down, head for the head, and then try a hot-start on an engine with vapor lock to get things going again toward your destination.

I didn't have the time. I was already dressed in my suit, and would be taken straight to the podium as soon as I landed.

Time for some problem solving. Clearly, I needed to find something in the cockpit into which I could rid myself of my... um... anxieties. It was a rental airplane—not like my own Mooney I fly today. So I had nothing—nothing except that can of Coca-Cola there on the right seat.

Hmm.

Well, there was still a problem: It was full of Coke. No help.

But, wait a minute! What if I was to drink the Coke?! Then, I would have an empty can and, by the time the Coke made its way through my system to cause even more problems, I would be safely on the ground at Jekyll.

Right?

So, pop the top and chug-a-lug! Time was a wastin'!

Now, the air was a bit bumpy that afternoon, and I was wearing a suit, so I wanted to be real careful here. Maybe it would be best just to pull my pants—skivvies and all—right down to my ankles, so that a bump wouldn't cause any embarrassing stains.

Yup, you're getting the picture and probably wishing you didn't.

Down go the pants, out comes the... well, you know... and soon we have a full Coke can in the cup holder.

Time to get dressed and land the airplane. Let's just say that here is where things went painfully wrong.

As I leaned over to grab my pants to pull them up, WHAM! There went the back. Muscle spasm. Not just a normal, run-of-the-mill back spasm, mind you. This was one of those slap-yo-mama spasms. One that brings tears to your eyes and the realization that you are going to look like a pretzel for a few days.

Instantly, I had a horrifying realization: I could not fly the airplane and pull those pants up. Too chancy, and the autopilot would only control heading. So, I followed the first rule of airmanship: Fly the airplane.

Soooooo... here he is, the Talkmaster, merrily approaching Jekyll Island—late in the afternoon, alone in a small airplane with his pants down around his ankles. *Not good.*

Focus.

Fly the airplane.

Finally, the Jekyll Island airport came into view. I got on the Unicom frequency to let other pilots know where I was and what I was doing (well, not *exactly* what I was doing), and greased one right on the centerline. I taxied over to the ramp and parked the airplane as far away from the airport's only building as I possibly could. Shutting down the engine, I turned off the master switch, took off the headphones, pushed the seat back, and got ready to pull those pants up.

I'm home free, right?

Now, little did I know that there was a completely over-eager kid working for flying lessons at the airport. His job was to help people with their luggage, tie down their airplanes, and put them in a little golf cart to take them to their car or the office.

So, there I am: Joe Pilot, nice suit—with my pants around my ankles when the door to the airplane yanks open.

Let's just say that there are some facial expressions you will never forget. Trust me, the look on the face of a teenaged boy as he opens the door to a small, single-engine airplane with only the pilot on board—and that pilot has clearly been flying with his pants down—is one you will remember for a long while.

The kid took one look, turned and *ran.*

There's not much more to tell. I yanked my pants up, stumbled out of the airplane, and found my ride to the hotel for my speech. A few aspirin and some stretching and, fortunately, I was good to go. The next morning, I left for Atlanta extra early, before the airport office opened for business.

I've never been back. I'm sure that there's a *Wanted* poster somewhere at that airport with my picture on it.

Come to think of it, maybe there is a 40-something-year-old man reading this book—a tormented man who used to tie down airplanes at the Jekyll Island airport as a teenager.

If so, yes, sir, that was me. I'm the guy with the pants down. I hope you weren't permanently scarred by the experience.

Oh and by the way: *The statute has expired.*

THE MAGICAL HARTSFIELD ELEVATOR INCIDENT

OK, I have to set the scene carefully for this story.

It's one of my favorites, but entirely visual and, in case you haven't noticed, there aren't any pictures in this book. Maybe this is one of those "you really had to be there" stories, but I'm going to try anyway.

The scene is Hartsfield International Airport. I know, they call it Hartsfield-Jackson International Airport now, but I honestly feel that the primary motive behind that was to make sure Atlanta's airport wasn't named after a white dude—or didn't *stay* named for a white dude. But that's just me…

Anyways…

When you travel from the gates to the main terminal, you either walk or ride a train through a mile-long tunnel that connects five concourses. This is, after all, the world's busiest airport. When you get to the end of that tunnel, there are three long escalators that take you up to the baggage claim and transportation level.

That's three long escalators, plus one elevator.

If you're waiting to pick someone up at the airport, you'll be standing at the top of the escalators watching the hoards of people head to baggage claim—where they will wait a minimum of 45 minutes—or out the door to their ride home.

Let me describe the scene at the top of the escalators: You have a throng of people standing behind a yellow line, waiting for their loved one, boss, escort, friend, *whatever*, to come gliding up.

Oh, and you have the elevator. Now this particular elevator (it has since been changed) is one with a door on both the front and the back. You enter the elevator from the back door, shall we say, and then exit through the front door when it reaches the baggage claim level.

There I was one evening, waiting for The Queen to return from her travels to yet another one of the world's exotic locales. (She has been to every continent except Antarctica.)

I'm not alone. There are perhaps 80 or so other people waiting to greet someone, too. Up comes the elevator, and the door opens.

Standing alone in the elevator is a businessman in a suit, carrying a briefcase, and wearing headphones. He's loving whatever music those headphones are playing, as he just stands there, doing a dance step.

No inhibitions, because he's the only one on the elevator. Let 'er rip, right? There's a problem, though. When he stepped into the elevator downstairs, he did what most of us do—he turned around to face the door.

Well, remember, that wasn't the door that was going to open when he got to the top. So, as Mr. Happy Feet does his little dance, never realizing that the door behind him is open, the elevator doors close and he heads back down. At the bottom, the elevator doors in front of him open.

He must have thought the elevator had gone nowhere, and he couldn't feel the movement because of his wonderful dance moves. So he pushes the button again, the door closes, and the elevator heads back up.

So there we still are when the elevator door opens yet again—and there is Mr. Dancing with the Stars just boogying away, headphones blaring and completely oblivious to the open door behind him.

Oh, the laughs coming from the crowd.

Door closes, and down he goes again.

The next time, we're waiting for him. About 45 seconds pass, the door opens, and Michael Flatley is still at it. But this time, the fine Atlanta cop who oversees this particular part of the airport is ready. He steps onto the elevator behind the unsuspecting dancing fool, and taps him on the shoulder.

You're remembering, aren't you? This guy thought he was on that elevator alone—and suddenly someone is tapping him on the shoulder. The briefcase goes flying into the air as Fred Astaire lets out a scream, spins around, and there are about 80 people laughing their arses off.

Give him credit.

He immediately sizes up the situation, picks up his briefcase, takes a bow, and walks off to the sound of applause.

I DON'T THINK
BILL O'REILLY LIKES
ME VERY MUCH

Is he talented? No doubt! Bill O'Reilly has one of the highest-rated shows on cable TV, so he must be doing something right. He writes bestseller after bestseller about killing presidents, and he can sell out an arena in about three-and-one-half minutes.

But interrupt? Good God! Can this man interrupt or what? If he had been on Mt. Eremos, he would have interrupted Jesus delivering his sermon.

O'Reilly used to be a school teacher. Can you imagine some poor kid in his class trying to answer a question? That school probably kept counselors on staff just to handle distraught kids from O'Reilly's classroom.

Well, you may have noticed that I haven't been on O'Reilly's show since May of 2003.[43] That was my one and only shot. There's a reason for that, and it's a story my listeners have asked me to tell over and over. I think that we can all agree that, if you manage to make His Haughtiness lose his cool on his own show, it's a fine moment, indeed.

To begin this little saga, we have to go back to April of 2003.

Bill O'Reilly is a generous man—generous enough to have contributed tens of thousands of dollars to a group called the Best Friends Foundation. This is a good group. They work with young men and women to build character and self-respect (the genuine type) by promoting self-control and good decision-making.

Well, on one particular day, O'Reilly was emceeing a benefit concert for the foundation. I'm guessing it was some sort of a talent show. At any rate, it came time for O'Reilly to introduce the next act—a group of young black children known as The Best Men.

Here's where he stepped in the puddin' just a bit. When O'Reilly introduced the act, they weren't there. Nobody walked out on the stage.

Not good.

So O'Reilly looked at the audience and expressed—out loud and into the microphone—a *live* microphone—that he sincerely hoped this group, The Best Men, weren't out there in the parking lot stealing everyone's hubcaps.

Oh! The humanity! How *raaaaaaaacist*!

Sure, Bill was trying to be funny. But there's a problem here: Only liberals are allowed to try to be funny with racial insensitivity. Hell, *everyone* knows that! Since our Bill isn't a liberal, all hell broke loose.

What to do?

Well, here's an idea! You could soothe some nerves and quiet the race warlords by showing what a champion you are to the downtrodden-and-forever-put-upon black community. That's just

---

[43]As a matter of fact, you haven't seen me on any Fox News Channel show for about the last six months. Not exactly sure why this is. I had been a regular guest of Megyn Kelly, Neil Cavuto and Judge Napolitano, as well as a few appearances on the curvy couch and even on Hannity for many years! Don't know what happened. Perhaps it was that jacket I wore on Cavuto one day. Maybe it was my sitting there gleefully spinning a Hannity football on the infamous day that Beckel dropped the "F-Bomb." Don't know why, but I'm about as welcome on Fox News Channel now as a canker sore at a Miss America contest.

what O'Reilly intended to do—all he needed was the right story.

He found one in Taylor County, Georgia. It was the story—completely untrue, mind you—of the all-white junior prom at Taylor County high in Butler, Georgia.

Butler isn't what you would call heavily populated, unless you consider 1,700 people a population-density crisis. The entire city covers only 3.2 square miles. Well, Butler is the county seat of Taylor County. Pull in the entire county and you have about 9,000 people.

Get the picture? This is *not* a partying kind of town.

Taylor High is so small that they generally forgo some of the usual events that make up a high-school year. At least, that's the way it was back in 2003.[44] So a group of Taylor High juniors decided they were going to have their own party.

Since there were no party facilities in Butler, they had to drive about 60 miles away to Columbus to find a cheap hotel ballroom worthy of their little soiree. This was not a school event—strictly a private party.

But, here's another problem—at least in the eyes of some local race hustlers. These Taylor High students didn't make sure to invite any—not even one—of their black classmates to this little party.

Naturally, you would expect someone's mama to get her panties in a wad over this, and that's just what happened. Thelma Thongsnapper, the mother of an aggrieved black student, set her hair on fire, got her bowels in an uproar and called the media, so suddenly we had a "Whites-Only Junior Prom" at Taylor High School—way down yonder in the middle of Jawjah.

Durned racist Juniors!

Haven't these kids been watching beer commercials or restaurant ads on TV? Everybody knows the rule is that you can never have a few people sitting around enjoying a cool one, unless at least

[44]If you want to see if Taylor High is having official proms now look it up on your own time. I'm trying to finish a book here, and this worthless little factoid is not important to my story.

one of those persons is black! What were these idiot kids thinking?

Ditto for restaurants! If a commercial shows a bunch of people going absolutely nutso over a stack of onion rings, one of those people had damned sure better be black or someone must have a serious racial problem.

I just don't know how these Taylor High kids missed this! C'mon now! It's the damned *law*!

Well, somehow O'Reilly found about the "Whites-Only Prom." *Ahhaaaa*! Redemption!

The evil white kids of Taylor County, Georgia came to rescue Bill O'Reilly from hubcap Armageddon! Here was a racial issue, albeit false, that O'Reilly could exploit to show what a friend of the oppressed he is!

Time to get busy.

O'Reilly actually talked Fox News Channel into sending a film crew down to Columbus to get some video of the whites-only prom. The students wouldn't comment, nor would the parents chaperoning the event. The students did, however, avail themselves of the presence of the cameras in order to practice their sign language.

"Hey O'Reilly! You're number one!"

O'Reilly then mounted his high horse (a swayback) and set off in search of comments from the school principal, the school superintendent, and Sonny Perdue, Georgia's governor.

Sadly, Perdue caved to racial political correctness and issued a statement saying he was "disappointed." Well, how very special. Perdue is disappointed that a group of white students decided to have a party—a private party—and they didn't invite any blacks.

Golly, Governor! So now it's the province of the top-elected official in the State of Georgia to pass on the guest list of all private parties in in the state and to then make a statement of pleasure or discontent as to the racial makeup of that list?

Now the truth is, O'Reilly knew this was a private party. He also knew that someone was stirring the racial puddin' by calling it a whites-only prom. But our pal Bill was badly in need of a good racial cause to champion, so facts went out the window and the spin was on!

Talk about shaky ground: Our hero went on TV and admitted it was a private party. Here, let O'Reilly tell you in his own words from his *Talking Points* memo:

> *"... so you come to school and find out some students in your class are holding an all-white prom. How would you react if you were that kid? You can't sue, because the event is being held off-campus. It's a private party, and no person of color is welcome. Yet the party is being held under the banner of Taylor High's junior prom. Yes, there is an alternative prom where everyone is welcome, but still a number of your classmates do not want to celebrate with you."*

Now let's see—in that one excerpt, O'Reilly admitted that this so-called prom was a private party.

I know I'm repeating myself, but this is an important point! O'Reilly chose the racial makeup of a guest list to a private party as the high ground he was going to occupy for the cause of addressing his current problems with the race warlords.

He admitted that there were no civil-rights violations that could give rise to a legal action. He admitted that the school itself did have a prom, though he called it an "alternative" prom. If it's the only prom being held by the school, how is that an "alternative" prom? O'Reilly didn't explain that one.

It seems that O'Reilly was making a big deal out of a private party held on private property, because they didn't invite any black kids.

But O'Reilly wasn't through. He went on to claim that the so-called whites-only prom actually was a school-sanctioned event.

Why?

Because the kids talked about it at school. They discussed plans and made arrangements when they saw each other in school.

Wow! So that makes it a school event? Then I guess when you invite the cute little girl in your homeroom out on a date, that's a school-sanctioned event, as well! After all, you invited her to the drive-in while you were both on school grounds, right?

You would have to be suffering from a severe case of rectal cranieitus[45] to buy that load of yak squeeze.

When O'Reilly did the segment on his show about the infamous Taylor County "Whites-Only" prom, he decided he needed a local guest. The governor sure wasn't going to talk to him and neither were any of the school officials. He tried to get the busboy who worked the party to talk, but he wasn't available.

So, in apparent desperation, he settled on me. *Yeah, we'll get that Neal Boortz guy down there in Atlanta and hammer him about this prom and see what he has to say.*

Bad mistake. I had done my homework—*all* of it. He didn't expect that.

So I made my way to the Fox News bureau on 14th Street in Atlanta, and got all glopped up with makeup.[46] I sat in that little chair in that dark little room with that Atlanta backdrop behind me, stared at that camera, and waited for my turn with The Great Interrupter.

O'Reilly started the segment in his usual fashion:

"Our next guest blah blah blah is an Atlanta talk show blah blah corn dogs blah blah host, Neal blah Boortz. Neal, these black blah blah get in the hole blah blah Taylor County blah blah Houston we have a problem blah blah blah whites only blah prom blah blah. What say you?"

I managed to get a word or two in.

"Bill, as you know, this was not a school-sanctioned event. These kids…"

"You're blah blah blah wrong and blah blah I used to be a teacher you know blah you blah blah know blah blah white racism blah blah mashed potatoes blah blah blah Megyn blah sanctioned by the blah blah unexcusable blah blah so you're wrong."

---

[45]Sometimes known as a "rectal-cranial inversion."

[46]I farded.

Time to drop the bomb.

"You know, Bill. It's clear what you're doing here. You're looking for some cover after that hubcap thing."

O'Reilly's eyes got wide. The left one started to bulge. His eyebrows shot up. He was changing colors quicker than a chameleon and steam was coming out of his ears. Cameramen were evacuating the studio.

A technician uttered the words, "Oh God!" in that little earpiece they had crammed into my ear. The great O'Reilly was beginning to look like he could explode. Then these words through clenched teeth:

"You are a vicious son-of-a-bitch!"

YES! That was on the air! O'Reilly was furious—he had been had! Exposed! He was going to pop a gasket.

Me? I was sitting there, laughing my butt off.

The interview ended.

Think about that: My one and only time on The O'Reilly Factor and he called me a vicious son of a bitch! I don't recall him ever calling anyone else that, so I really must be something special!

His name calling was not going to go unchallenged. I decided I would exact my revenge the next day on the air—I just had to figure out how.

As it turned out, news of my little encounter with O'Reilly preceded me to the air the next day. The listeners were ready.

We spent some time talking about O'Reilly's name-calling on my show the next day, but frankly I was more interested in setting the record straight on this absurdity about a whites-only prom. You can't just waltz up to a private party and decide on your very own that it's a prom and then go on national TV stirrin' the porridge this way. There had to be retribution—I just needed to come up with something.

Aha! Just what was it that O'Reilly was so worried about when The Best Men didn't show up for their act at the concert? Stealing hubcaps, wasn't it? Were Bill's hubcaps missing? Was there something we could do to make this thing all right for him?

Why certainly there was! We needed to get O'Reilly some hubcaps—yup, some emergency back-up hubcaps for Mr. No-Spin, in case his are stolen by a renegade group of 11-year-old rappers who managed to get their hands on some bad Kool Aid.

Oh, how I love my listeners. On that day, they came through, as I knew they would. I explained that O'Reilly seemed to be having a hubcap problem and "perhaps you could make things all better for our friend Bill if you send him a hubcap or two—maybe even sign them as loyal fans." I shared the address for Bill O'Reilly at Fox News Channel.

Well – share they did. The hubcaps (I don't know how many) arrived in New York, and I got a call from an O'Reilly producer telling me to knock this *blah blah* the *blah blah* hell off *blah blah* or else. Let me tell you, I was petrified.

That was about it. I waited by my phone for weeks for a return invite to the O'Reilly Factor.

It's now nine-and-a-half years later, and still no invite. Oh darn.

O'Reilly really needs to learn a lesson from Phil Donahue.

I was on Donahue's program once and got a little irritated—well, MORE than irritated—at being ignored. They had invited me there, so include me in the show, dammit! Finally, I just calmly took off the mic during a break and walked out of the studio without saying a word.

A few weeks later, we got a call from a Donahue producer. Donahue wished for me to know that never in his career had anyone walked out on him, and this simply was not going to stand. I was invited to fly to New York, on their dime, spend a night in one of those fancy NYC hotels, again on their dime, and be Phil's solo guest for an entire hour on live TV before a studio audience.

I accepted. Flew to New York. Did the show. And Donahue was promptly cancelled a few days later.

Good Lord! *I killed the man's show!*

Maybe O'Reilly would be better off if he continues to ignore me. Another encounter just wouldn't work out all that well at all.

I'm retiring—nothing to lose. And you *know* I love to speak my mind.

I DON'T THINK THE STATE OF VIRGINIA LIKES ME ALL THAT MUCH, EITHER.

Well, at least there are some members of the Virginia Assembly, or legislature, or circus—or whatever you call it—who aren't too fond of the Talkmaster.

This particular saga started with the tragic shootings on the campus of Virginia Tech. On April 16, 2007, Seung-Hui Cho shot and killed 32 people and wounded 15 others. There were actually two separate attacks, separated by about two hours. You can go online and read the accounts of the shootings.

Students in various classrooms tried to barricade the doors—but, if you read the accounts, that was pretty much the extent of any efforts at self defense.

OK, here's where I made people mad. Not just mad—I mean blue-steam, trembling mad. *Furious* doesn't describe it.

There was, as you might expect, a great deal of conversation on the air about the Virginia Tech shooting. Most of the conversation revolved around what we should be doing by way of stricter gun control. Some who discussed the idea of allowing adult students with concealed carry permits to carry guns on campus were shouted down as gun nuts and lunatics.

Several days, perhaps a week after the shooting, the conversation was still hot and heavy on the air. Still, the debate centered on gun control and concealed-weapons permits. But there was something bothering me about the shootings that just wasn't being articulated in the conversation.

Finally, I just had to get it out.

There was a legitimate question to be asked, and it needed to be asked sooner rather than later: *Why?*

Why, when the shooter had to pause several times during his 2-1/2 hour rampage to either change guns or reload—*why*, during the time it took this lunatic to shoot and kill 32 people and wound 15 more—*why*, during this entire episode, *didn't just ONE person rush this guy?*

Why didn't just one person, let alone a group, attack this person from behind? Why, while he was breaking down a barricade down and coming through a door, didn't anyone resist?

Did these people just sit around, some behind barricades, waiting for their turn to be shot? There didn't seem to be one student or faculty member who thought, "Well, I'm probably going to get shot, anyway, so I might as well attack this guy to see if I can save my life and the lives of some others."

Now I didn't come to this question out of the blue clear sky. I recalled another school shooting about two years earlier on the Red Lake Indian Reservation in Minnesota. There is no need to get into the gory details of this shooting. This is supposed to be, for the most part, a fun book.

Suffice it to say that some deranged kid by the name of Jeffrey Weise took some guns, killed his grandfather and his grandfather's girlfriend, and headed to the Red Lake Senior High School. As he entered the school, he started shooting. He shot and killed a security guard at the school entrance and then went on a killing spree inside the school.

Weise entered the classroom of Neva Jane Winnecoup-Rogers, an English teacher. He shot and killed her as he entered the classroom. As Weise shot and killed three students, wounding three others, an overweight, 16-year-old sophomore by the name of Jeff May (yup, same first name) decided that he was not going to just sit there and wait to be shot. Nor was he going to do nothing while more of his classmates were gunned down.

He had no weapon—only the pencil he was holding in his hand when Weise entered the classroom. If that's all May had to use as a weapon, so be it. He charged Weise and attempted to stab him in the abdomen with the pencil. Weise was wearing a Kevlar vest and the pencil broke.

May was shot three times, once in the jaw, but it didn't stop him. He wrestled Weise to the ground and struggled with him, while the rest of the students evacuated the classroom. Faced with a now-empty classroom, Weise left May for dead on the floor and proceeded to the front of the school where he got into a firefight with police officers.

After suffering a few gunshot wounds from the police, Weise put the shotgun he was carrying in his mouth and pulled the trigger. DRT.

Nobody really knows how many lives Jeff May saved that day. Some say at least eight, the number of kids who escaped the classroom. Others say more. May is to this day still working to recuperate from his wounds.

But there you go, folks. On the Red Lake Indian Reservation, we have a pudgy 16-year-old hero who charges a shooter with a pencil and saves God knows how many lives. At Virginia Tech, we had classrooms full of people older than 16, some of whom were presumably in good shape, and not one mounted an assault on Seung-Hui Cho.

All I did was say so.

Well, as you might expect, not a whole helluva lot of time passed before I was being ripped to shreds across the Internet for daring to ask such an incredibly insensitive question. How DARE I question why these students and faculty members didn't do something to defend themselves? Apparently, self defense is such an outmoded concept in this country that the mere mention of the idea brings howls of outrage.

Of course, much of the outrage against me was manufactured by various left-wing Internet sites and bloggers who are dedicated more to the idea of destroying those who express opinions that differ from theirs than they are to open discussion.

So it was then, so it shall ever be—until, that is, they succeed in totally outlawing the expression of conservative or Libertarian ideas on the "public's airwaves."

Oh, wait.

So where does the Virginia legislature come in? The controversy over that evil right-wing nut-job Neal Boortz suggesting that someone—anyone—at Virginia Tech might have actually wanted to consider an act of self defense spilled over to the Virginia legislature.

Three members of that august body actually introduced a resolution demanding that all radio stations in Virginia that carry my show immediately stop.

No more Neal Boortz on Virginia radio!

The radio stations, of course, had a better grasp of the principles set forth in the First Amendment than those idiots did, so nothing happened. No station dropped my show.

Me? I started counting down the days until I once again said something that many people were thinking, but were afraid to express, and the howling dogs of the left-wing media would once again rise up in outrage.

I could hardly wait.

AND THE PEOPLE OF NEW ORLEANS HAVE STOPPED SENDING ME CHRISTMAS CARDS.

I mentioned earlier that Royal, Belinda and I were in New Orleans the very day before Katrina struck. I can still remember the mad dash to the airport to see if we could make one of the last flights out. We did, thankfully.

In the days that followed, we watched in complete shock with the rest of the country at the drama unfolding in New Orleans. It wasn't really the hurricane winds that all but killed the city. It was the levees failing and the city being inundated with water.

The planning for this disaster in New Orleans was less than inept. Then Mayor Ray Nagle and Governor Kathleen Blanco were about as effective in their leadership of the rescue efforts as Obama has been in creating jobs. That translates into total incompetence and ineffectiveness.

I'm sure you remember, as I do, the scenes of chaos as National Guardsmen and other rescue agencies tried to evacuate people from bridges, rooftops, and pretty much anywhere they could go to escape the flood.

The busses were lining up to take these Katrina refugees to other major cities, Houston among them. I began my controversial comments on Katrina and New Orleans with the warning, "Houston, you have a problem."

I warned my fellow Texans that the type of people being bussed to Houston weren't exactly pillars of the New Orleans community, and that there was going to be a price to pay. Sure enough, mere weeks later, Houston schools started to experience gang violence from displaced New Orleans gangs, and Houston businesses registered an uptick in petty and more serious crimes.

And so it goes.

This whole rescue, evacuation and relocation process got me to thinking. That can be dangerous, because it leads sometimes to thoughts—perfectly rational thoughts—that one just shouldn't express in polite company.

"Save the rich people first."

There. I said it. It was out there. And let me tell you, you have nooooooo idea how absolutely furious that made some of my listeners.

I tried to explain myself. It went something like this:

"Look, you may not like it, but you have to face reality here. After the cleanup from Katrina is over, after the levees have been rebuilt, and after the flood waters have receded, you're going to be faced with a monumental rebuilding task. Housing is going to have to be restored and rebuilt. Businesses will have to be put back on their feet, again. You're going to need people with the brains, the abilities, the work ethic, and the resources to bring these businesses and the jobs they provide back to The Crescent City.

"Do you think poor people are going to be able to do all this? Do you really think the great welfare class (one of the nation's largest) of New Orleans is going to suddenly develop the skills, the resources and the ability to rebuild this city? Perhaps the rescuers ought to pay some attention to finding and saving the people who will have the wherewithal to rebuild New Orleans. Those people are probably rich. Save them. Perhaps you might want to save them first."

The reality, of course, is that you rescue people as you come upon them, without regard to wealth, race or class status. There was a point to be made, though. Some of the Katrina refugees were going to do absolutely nothing positive to rebuild New Orleans or any city to which they are evacuated after the storm. They've lived their lives as parasites, and parasites they would remain. Insensitive? Yup!

That's pretty insensitive, but so is life. Deal with it.

I'm speaking the truth here, and the listeners knew it. Others, the productive and achievement-oriented citizens of New Orleans, were going to hit the ground running to rebuild. They were not going to sit around complaining about insufficient services from government or The Red Cross. They were going to roll up their sleeves and get to work.

Save 'em first. The city would only benefit.

Aftermath? Well, first of all, the station carrying my show in New Orleans cancelled my show. I suppose that was inevitable. After all, I was no more welcome there than John Wilkes Booth at the Ford Theatre after that Lincoln incident.

The truth hurts, my friends, and that one was painful. But it was the truth.

IRINI

There are some stories from the last 42 years that just must be told. They may not necessarily be about talk radio, but these experiences did result from my career.

The story of Irini is one that I just have to tell, because this story, possibly more than any other in my arsenal, illustrates the greatness of our country, especially as seen in the eyes of a foreigner.

Irini Notkin[47] is married to Russian broadcaster Boris Notkin. Donna and I went on a Friendship Force trip to Russia in 1991 and were privileged to stay in their home in Moscow.

Even though Boris, sometimes called Russia's Ted Koppel, was one of the most recognized television personalities in Russia, he and Irini lived a very meager life by American standards. Their

---

[47]Sure hope I'm spelling her name right. Did the research. Sent the emails. No response, and couldn't find her name in print. Phonetic pronunciation Eye-reen-eee.

apartment featured a small kitchen, which is where they ate meals, a living room, a bedroom and a tiny bath.

There was so little space that they had to hang clothes on the shower curtain rod in the bathroom. You would move them when you took a shower. I would guess this all added up to about 800 square feet—and this was for one of Russia's biggest TV stars with 40 million viewers to his twice-weekly show.

While Donna and I were visiting, Boris and Irini moved into a hide-a-bed in the living room and gave us their bedroom to sleep.

The Notkins were not alone with these cramped living quarters. They took us to visit Moscow neighbors who had children. Their place was so small that the kids had to sleep on two sets of bunk beds in the kitchen. Most poor people in the U.S. at this time had far better living conditions than Boris and Irini.

We took this family and the kids to the new McDonalds that had just opened in Moscow for some good ol' American food. Don't hold me to the figures, but I think Donna and I spent about 47 rubles buying the family hamburgers, fries and milkshakes. Irini took us aside to tell us that we had just spent more on that one McDonalds meal than this family made in an entire month.

Quite the worker's paradise.

One evening—one I shall never forget—Irini decided she was going to cook a meal for us at home. I soon learned that cooking a meal at home for a Russian family, even a Russian family with status, was quite a bit more involved than what we typically experience in America. Irini asked me if I would like to go with her to pick up some things she needed for the dinner.

Of course, I said yes.

We bundled up against the cold—it was the middle of winter—and headed out with some shopping bags to essentially forage for some food.

Did we head out to some local grocery store?

Are you kidding me? Grocery store? *Hardly.*

The first stop was a bakery. Maybe it wasn't actually a bakery—let's just say they sold bread. The store was dark and cold, and the shelves contained perhaps a half-dozen baguettes of bread—rock-hard bread. Irini selected a loaf, and we went off in search of some meat.

Bear in mind that we were slogging through frozen slush and mud from dark-and-empty store to dark-and-empty store. Finally, we found a shop with a few cuts of meat. I'm only guessing about the species, but I *think* it was cow meat. We bought a small hunk of apparent beef and headed out in search of vegetables.

Absolutely no luck there. No veggies to be found.

We headed back to the Notkin apartment, where Irini put her heart and soul into preparing dinner for us. Visitors from America! She wanted so badly to impress—and impress us she did. It was not necessarily because of the quality and quantity of the food, but with the effort and love she put into the preparation. We ate heartily and Irini seemed pleased.

Then Magda, their schnauzer, bit me. *But that's another story.*

Though her husband, Boris, had traveled extensively around the world as a speaker on Soviet and Russian issues, Irini had never been past the Soviet and then Russian border.

That was about to change.

The Friendship Force, you see, was an exchange program. On that particular trip to Moscow, we were among the first American families to actually visit Russia and live with Russian citizens. On a previous visit, when it was the Soviet Union, not The Russian Federation, we were restricted to hotels—hotels where Soviet citizens dared not go.

About six months after our visit to Irini and Boris in Moscow, they came to visit us in Atlanta. Our Moscow hosts flew to Atlanta with several hundred other Russians on what was the second part of this Friendship Force exchange.

The Delta Airlines L1011 was pulled into a hangar at Atlanta's Hartsfield airport before our Russian guests disembarked. About 80 host families from Georgia were there to greet them, including Donna and I waiting for Boris and Irini.

I'm not going to go in depth describing Irini's reactions as we drove through the streets of Atlanta on our way home. This was her first view of an American city, and she was in awe. She asked us if those were rich Americans with all the cars.[48]

Their flight had been a long one, so they wanted to head straight to our house and crash. They had been fed on the flight, so dinner was not an issue.

The next day I saw something—something in Irini's eyes—that I shall never forget as long as I live. Remembering Irini's home-cooked meal in Moscow, it was decided that we would have dinner at home that night. We would barbecue a couple of steaks, roast some corn-on-the-cob and fix a nice green salad.

So it was that Donna, Irina and I climbed into the car and headed to a place called Harry's Farmer's Market. I can best describe Harry's by comparing it to today's Whole Food stores, except that the produce section was perhaps three times as large.

Frankly, I wasn't thinking about my slog through the Moscow frozen slush and mud on our shopping trip for dinner six months before. I might not have been, but Irini was.

The trip to Harry's was just a normal shopping trip—get in, get your stuff, get out. We went through the front door—you know the routine—grabbed a cart and headed into the store.

After about 15 steps, I felt a tap on my shoulder. It was Donna. She pointed back toward the door.

There stood Irini.

She was frozen in place. Staring.

This is something every American had seen before—seen thousands of times—the American grocery store, a huge farmer's market.

I walked up to Irini, and then I saw it: There were tears streaming down her cheeks. She was crying. Not crying out of sorrow, but crying at the wonderment of it all.

---

[48]The Notkins had a car. A very small one. It was stored in a ramshackle, single-car garage about three blocks from their apartment. Having a car in Russia at that time was quite the status symbol. A garage where you lived to park it? Unheard of.

She had been raised to believe that the average American lived in abject oppression and poverty and that only the rich enjoyed a life of plenty. In the time it took to walk into a grocery store, she learned that it was all a lie. Life in America was not what she had been led to believe.

In Irini's eyes that night, I saw the wonder of freedom and economic liberty. I saw the tears of recognition of what happens when people are turned loose, free of the restraints of the political class and despotic rulers, to pursue their goals and their dreams.

If only Americans could see a grocery store with the same eyes that Irini Notkin saw that farmer's market over 20 years ago.

Sadly, the average American today would be more likely to complain about what they didn't see on those shelves and bins ("Where's my favorite creamed corn?") than in what Irini did see—the wonder of America's free market economy.

That free market economy is now under attack. We have a president who was raised to despise free enterprise. To Barack Obama, capitalism has always been a tool of oppression. With every year of his presidency that passes, America moves further and further down the list of countries rated on their degree of economic liberty.

If I live long enough, and if the moochers, parasites and leaches keep electing people like Obama to our nation's highest office, one day I'll visit a Russian grocery store—and stand there with tears in my eyes at the wonder of it all.

MY SIMPLY AMAZING CITIZENSHIP TEST

In the mid 2000s, I made a trip to Asheville, North Carolina to stay at the Grove Park Inn over the Fourth of July holiday.

Asheville is stunning, a beautiful place, but somehow it has suffered an infestation of liberals. Those people just seem to feed on each other's perceived sense of intellectual superiority.

Asheville is indeed a great place to visit, if you take great joy in scandalizing the locals with well-placed, evil right-wing snarky comments—something I've always enjoyed.

Example? You see a woman walking a dog in Asheville. Chances are way better than good that she's a proggie.

"Excuse me, ma'am, but you do have a bag to pick up those little Democrats your dog is depositing, don't you?

So while I was in Asheville, I picked up a copy of the local proggie poop sheet, *The Asheville Citizen-Times*. Right there, on the front page, they had their version of a "Citizenship Test" for Independence Day.

How patriotic!

The questions were real crushers, too! Who is the governor of North Carolina? When was the Declaration of Independence signed? What is the North Carolina State Motto?

Really? This is a citizenship test? If I know the motto of the State of North Carolina, I'm a good informed citizen?

Whisky Tango Foxtrot!

So when I got back home from that little junket to Asheville, I decided to sit down and fix this Bolshoi by writing a real citizenship test.

I first posted it, along with some snarky comments about *The Asheville Citizen-Times*, on my blog at Boortz.com. Then the test was refined and made its way into my book *Somebody's Gotta Say It*.

At that point, something interesting happened: I started getting letters and emails from teachers and home-schooling parents around the country, asking me if they could give my citizenship test to their students.

Why, of course! Be my guest!

Since this may be my last real chance to put *The Neal Boortz Citizenship Test* in front of thousands of additional American school children, not to mention their parents and teachers, I've made some revisions to bring this test up to speed.

Feel free to copy this and to give it to your students or kids. Make it an open-book test. Require no less than a 100-word answer to each question. For some questions, you may want to require more.

Trust me, your students will learn more about their country by spending a few days or a week coming up with answers to this quiz than they will learn in an American civics or history classroom for the rest of the year.

While we're at it, it wouldn't be such a bad idea if some of you journalists, pundits and talk show hosts reading this book took a stab at this test as well. You may be surprised about how little you know—or about how much you know that just ain't so.

And for you parents, before you give it to your kids, maybe you want to take it yourself. That way, you're ready to help your kids when they come to you for help.

You will look SOOOO wise. It can't hurt.

THE TALKMASTER'S CITIZENSHIP TEST

1. Forget when the Declaration of Independence was signed. (Hint: It wasn't July 4.) Instead, explain why it was signed. What were the signers trying to accomplish?
2. What happened to the men who signed the Declaration? Did they go on to be heroes and live happily ever after?
3. Neal Boortz is a direct descendant of one of the signers of the Declaration of Independence. Go to ancestry.com and see if you can figure out which one. Hint: A slave-owner
4. During the Revolutionary War, were the majority of colonists in favor of independence from England?
5. What does the Declaration of Independence say the people can do on their own when a government becomes destructive to the ends of liberty?
6. Regarding No. 6, are we almost there?
7. What would happen to anyone who tried today to alter or abolish our government if it became destructive to the idea that government derives its powers from the consent of the governed?
8. Which articles of the Constitution grant specific powers to the federal government?
9. Which article of the Constitution restricts the powers of the government to only those specifically set forth in the Constitution?
10. Which article of the Constitution do you think is most often ignored by the Congress of the United States? Why would that happen?
11. Forget the words. Just describe the circumstances under

which Francis Scott Key wrote the words to "The Star Spangled Banner."

12. Do you believe people living in a free country ought to be compelled to recite a pledge of allegiance to that country?

13. Why?

14. If you are required to recite a pledge of allegiance, are you really free?

15. Should Washington have developed an "exit strategy" before he ever led his troops into battle during the Revolutionary War?

16. Where in our Constitution is it stated that anyone has a right to vote for the office of President of the United States? (If you've been following me, this one's a gift.)

17. How did our original Constitution provide for the appointment of United States Senators?

18. Most foreign countries appoint an ambassador to be their official representative before the federal government of the United States. Who officially represents the 50 state governments before the government of the United States?

19. Explain the difference between a rule of law and the rule of man.

20. Explain the difference between a democracy and a constitutional republic.

21. Was our country founded as a country of majority rule?

22. Can you imagine what our country would be like today if the majority did rule?

23. Aren't you glad the majority doesn't rule?

24. If two wolves and one sheep vote on what they're going to have for dinner, what do you think the menu will look like?

25. How many times can the word "democracy" be found in the Declaration of Independence and the U.S. Constitution?

26. How many times can the word "democracy" be found in the constitutions of any of the 50 states?

27. What does this tell you?

28. Was the word "Democrat" ever considered to be an epithet?

(I mean in our past. Of course it's an epithet now.)

29. Define "civil war."

30. Was the war between the Northern and Southern states in the mid-1800s a civil war?

31. Did Lincoln's Emancipation Proclamation really free the slaves? All of them?

32. Where in our Constitution does it say that black people are only 3/5ths of a real person?

33. What was the Missouri Compromise?

34. Write three 100-word paragraphs: One defining racism, one defining bigotry, and the final paragraph defining prejudice.

35. Try to remember everything you did yesterday—everybody you met or encountered. Everybody with whom you interacted. List the number of times you profiled during the day.

36. Who is third in the line of succession to the presidency?

37. How did the political class manage to fool the people of the United States into supporting a Constitutional Amendment creating an income tax?

38. How do most people get their news on a daily basis?

39. Does the "freedom of the press" clause in the First Amendment apply to the broadcast media?

40. Do most people get their news from agencies licensed to operate by the federal government? Explain.

41. Why were the words "under God" placed into the Pledge of Allegiance?

42. Do you think it's proper for the federal government to compel students attending government schools under compulsory attendance laws to acknowledge the role of God in the formation of our country? Would this constitute "effecting an establishment of religion"? If not, why not?

43. Has any federal court ever ruled that children cannot pray in government schools?

44. Do Americans, as Bill Clinton once said, derive their basic rights from the Constitution?

45. If we don't derive our rights from the Constitution, just why

was the Bill of Rights added, anyway?

46. Define a system of government where the means of production are owned and controlled privately.

47. Define a system of government where the means of production are privately owned but controlled by government.

48. Define a system of government where the means of production are owned and controlled by the government.

49. Why do liberals have such a tough time answering question number 42?

50. What does your annual income have to be to become one of the top 1 percent in America?

51. What percentage of total income is earned by the top 1 percent of income earners?

52. What percentage of total income taxes collected by the federal government is paid by the top 1 percent of income earners?

53. Where in our Constitution does it specifically state that only U.S. citizens may vote for the office of President of the United States? (Caution: *trick question*)

54. Name one right that a state government can exercise without interference from the federal level. Good luck with this one.

55. Where in our Constitution does it specifically state that only U.S. citizens may vote for members of the House of Representatives?

56. Look at the Bill of Rights. List any amendments in the Bill of Rights that were ratified for the purpose of limiting the powers of the government.

57. Next list all amendments in the Bill of Rights that actually grant powers to the federal government.

58. If our Constitution provides for equal protection under the law, why does the Voting Rights Act only apply to certain states that were held in political disfavor in the 1970s?

59. List any amendments in the Bill of Rights that were ratified for the purpose of limiting the rights of individuals.

60. If the Bill of Rights was written to limit the rights of government and to guarantee certain rights to the individual, try to explain why so many people seem to think that the Second Amendment was written to limit the rights of individuals and guarantee the rights of government.

61. Does the First Amendment protect speech that some people might find offensive?

62. Explain how our republic was threatened when Janet Jackson showed the world that she likes to wear a Japanese throwing star on the nipple of her left breast.

63. What is the one exclusive power our government has that no individual or business can legally exercise?

64. If we were playing rock-paper-scissors and treaties with foreign nations duly ratified by our Senate were the paper, would our Constitution be the rock or the scissors?

65. Do you have the right to use force to take money from a stranger if you tell the stranger you are mugging that you're going to give that money to someone in need?

66. Explain the concept of our government deriving its powers from the consent of the governed.

67. Now explain how you can tell the government to do something for you that, if you did it for yourself, would be a crime.

68. Regarding the 2000 presidential election, two questions:
    (a) Did the Supreme Court order the State of Florida to stop its recount of the vote?
    (b) Did the Supreme Court declare George W. Bush to be the winner of the election?

69. Should the government make something you might do a crime if that action doesn't violate another person's right to life, liberty, or property through force or fraud?

70. How many votes must you have in the Senate to be assured that a piece of legislation will pass?

71. Do you have a choice as to whether or not you pay Social Security taxes?

72. Why, then, do they call Social Security taxes "contributions?"

73. What is the average age of a country or society based on the rule of law and guaranteeing freedom, individual rights, and economic liberty?

74. Has the United States outlived its life expectancy?

75. Explain what a capital gains tax is, and why capital gains are taxed at a lower rate than earned income.

76. True or False: Warren Buffet pays exactly the same capital gains taxes on the same capital gains as does his secretary.

77. True or False: Warren Buffett pays exactly the same income taxes on the same taxable income as does his secretary.

78. Was Barack Obama lying when he said Warren Buffet pays a lower tax rate than his secretary?

79. In 2012, Barack Obama ran against Mitt Romney for another term as president. Regarding Obama and Romney, which one wrote in their autobiography that the private sector was the "enemy?"

80. Which 2012 presidential candidate, Mitt Romney or Barack Obama, announced his entry into the world of politics from the living room of a convicted domestic terrorist?

81. Did Sarah Palin ever say that she could see Russia from her house? If so, cite the date. If not, explain just exactly what Sarah Palin did say.

82. Has there ever been a day during Obama's first term as president when more Americans had jobs than on the last day of George W. Bush's presidency?

83. Did Barack Obama reduce our deficit during his first term in office?

84. Is it a crime to illegally enter this country?

85. Explain why it is bad to call someone who has committed an illegal act, like entering this country illegally, illegal.

If I didn't have so many other things to cover, I could expand this list until it filled an entire book. For instance, I could add a hundred or so questions beginning with "Where does the United States Constitution give the federal government the right to . . ."

I think 85 questions are enough, though, don't you?

Here's a fun fact: Within days, after I first posted this revised citizenship test on my website on July 5, 2006, I was flooded with letters and messages from government-school teachers around the nation, telling me that this quiz, and the matters covered therein, would be the core of their next history and/or government class.

That's nice to know, and I thank them for the affirmation. As for the rest of you, it might be interesting to spend one class session asking these questions.

Who knows? Someone might accidentally learn something.

OSCAR, EMMY, TONY, GUGLIEMO AND RUSH

Movies have the Oscars. For TV performers, it's the Emmys. The Broadway types have their Tonys. For those of us in radio, it's the Marconi's.

I couldn't tell you how Oscar got his name. Nor can I tell you Emmy or Tony's last name. Marconi? That's good ol' Gugliemo. He's the guy—Italian, if you can't tell—who invented long-distance radio transmissions.

The Marconi Awards are handed out every year by the National Association of Broacasters. Getting a Marconi is just about as good as it gets in broadcasting—except for one other award. We'll get to that in a moment.

Just as with the other awards I mentioned, there are many categories and many chances to win a Marconi. While most of the awards are actually given to radio stations, there are chances for individuals to take one home. You can be the best small, medium, large or major market radio personality, for instance.

My colleague Scott Slade won the award for Major Market Personality of the Year in 2006, and the mothership, WSB, won the legendary Station of the Year award in 2002.

There's one more individual award—for the network/syndicated personality of the year.

I can't remember exactly what year it was that I became, for the first time, a finalist for Syndicated Personality of the Year. I believe the NAB convention was being held in Los Angeles that year, so I dutifully grabbed the Queen and headed off to La La Land for the awards banquet.

I didn't win.

The second time (again, trying to drag this out of my memory), the convention was in Seattle. Once more, I trundled across the country to eat some stale bread and watch someone else take the award.

Third time? Charlotte, North Carolina. At least this time, I only had to travel a few hundred miles to applaud the winner—who was not me.

There's a reason I simply could not manage to win a Marconi. The nomination process was based on your successes in the various markets you served through syndication, a somewhat subjective process.

The actual award was based on one thing and one thing only—votes.

NAB station managers and program directors received a ballot with the names of the nominees and cast their votes. Simple math. The nominee with the most stations in syndication was always going to beat a nominee with a significantly smaller number of subscribing radio stations. Talent and ratings had little to do with it.

I was never one of the big boys in the talk radio world. Limbaugh has about 600 stations. Hannity? Around 500. Me? I peaked at about 240 or so.

Now I need to interject something here about the difference in the way Hannity and I handled our relationships with our affiliate stations. Sean could tell you the name of every station manager and program director for every single station that carried his show. What's more, he knew their birthdays, their spouses' names, the breeds, gender, age and names of their dogs and the names of all of their children.

I mean, this guy worked it.

He would call the manager of the smallest station that carried his show on exactly the right day of the school year to say, "Just wondering, Clarence. Did little Cosmo get a better math score on this report card? I sure hope that book I sent him helped."

I'm not in the slightest being disparaging here. Hannity is probably the hardest worker in talk radio. Me? Um, no. I just did the best show I could possibly do and, if that was good enough for the stations, fine. If not… well, I'm sorry, I tried. Name all these station managers? Are you kidding?

But this chapter isn't about Hannity. It's about Rush Limbaugh. I know—how in the world did I lurch from Marconi Awards to Rush Limbaugh just like that? Here's the story:

After my third Marconi wipeout, I told the radio station that I did not ever want to be nominated for a Marconi, again. I appreciated the effort they put into those nominations. Really, I did. But the simple fact was the numbers weren't there and I was going to just keep burning kerosene to get to these NAB meetings to hear someone else's name called.

That brings us to Rush—a multiple Marconi Award winner, as you might guess. I can't remember when this happened, but several years ago—perhaps 10 years ago—Rush told me that if I was ever made a member of the Radio Hall of Fame in Chicago, he would like to deliver the induction speech. That was likely an easy promise to make at the time, because how in the world was I going to be named to the Hall of Fame?

But after my third Marconi loss, and after telling the station promotion people to drop all future plans to throw my name into that hat, anymore, I started thinking about the Hall of Fame.

Perhaps it was just to save face, but I told The Queen and my friends at the radio station that, though it was clear I would never win a Marconi, I would really consider it an honor to be named to the Hall of Fame while I was still on the right side of the grass. Vertical, if you will.

I never said anything else about it—but apparently some folks went to work. In 2009, I was notified that I had been nominated for the National Radio Hall of Fame—and I was still drawing breath!

A few months later, the news came: I was in! I was going to be inducted into the Radio Hall of Fame!

My first thought was that someday my granddaughter would be able to visit the Hall of Fame in Chicago, point to my picture, and tell her children that this is their Great-Grandpa. I couldn't have been more thrilled. This meant so much more to me than a Marconi!

No doubt it would be the Number One moment of my entire career. Imagine! A guy fired from his first radio job for turning 100 tarantulas loose in a studio in the Hall of Fame.

Only in America!

As soon as I got the word, I thought of Rush. Was he serious when he said he wanted to deliver my induction speech? After all, that promise had been made five or six years earlier. Well, what the hell. I was going to find out.

So I sent Rush an email telling him of my honor and reminding him of his promise. I gave him every out I could dream up, but casually mentioned, "Just in case, I thought I would let you know."

Many weeks went by without hearing anything back from Rush. Sean Hannity called to ask if he could deliver the speech— a wonderful gesture. I told him of Rush's promise and that I had contacted him, but had not yet heard back. Sean told me that he would be the backup, in case Rush demurred.

We were just a few weeks away from the Hall of Fame ceremonies in Chicago when I finally heard from Rush. It seemed that the induction ceremony was being held on a Saturday night, smack dab in the middle of his annual golf outing with friends in Palm Beach, Florida. Rush explained to me that this was the very weekend he had invited a cadre of friends to stay with him for three days of golf and some great dining.

He went on to explain that he was going to play golf on Saturday, have someone else host the Saturday evening dinner, and fly up to Chicago to deliver the speech! He would then return to Palm Beach that night to be ready for his tee time on Sunday Morning.

I was honored and thrilled. This was going to be quite an evening!

A few days before the ceremony, I received another message from Rush. It seemed that he had explained his plans for that Saturday night to his golfing guests, and many of them were fans of the show. They wanted to come, too! Rush was warning me that there would be a few extra bodies tagging along for the evening.

Fine with me! *The more the merrier!*

The magic night came: November 7, 2009. About 30 minutes before the ceremony, Rush came walking into the Chicago Renaissance Hotel with his golfing friends—baseball Hall of Famer George Brett, PGA celebrity announcer and mustache model Gary McCord, and author and creator of Mitch Rapp, Vince Flynn.

Rush was dressed in some sort of a herringbone creation from Loudmouth Clothes. Perhaps you've seen golfer John Daley wear some of Loudmouth's more subtle creations. Or maybe you saw me wearing my own Loudmouth sports coat during my last appearance on Neil Cavuto's show on Fox News Channel. That jacket, I believe, is what led to my ultimate blacklisting from all but Hannity's show on Fox.[49]

That night, Rush Limbaugh showed me that he is solid gold. He made a promise, and then kept that promise when it was horribly inconvenient to do so. I know a little bit about flying, and I'm guessing that the cost of flying that Gulfstream G-4 to Chicago and back would come in somewhere around $35,000 to $40,000. I will

---

[49]Then again, I was there, sitting on the Hannity panel, the night Bob Beckel dropped the "F-Bomb." I just sat there in complete indifference, tossing one of Hannity's footballs in the air. Go to YouTube—you'll find it. Haven't been invited back. Somebody had to pay, I guess.

never be able to thank Rush enough for the kindness and generosity he showed that night—not to mention the fact that he had done for talk radio what Arnold Palmer had done for golf, lifting talk radio to a level that enabled me to quit the practice of law to make my living taking phone calls.

The National Hall of Fame award is now displayed in the BoortzBus. It will be the only memento of my radio career that The Queen and I will carry on our travels around the country. I give my profound thanks to the people who cast their ballots for me in 2009.

The Marconi saga, however, was not over.

Though I had asked them to refrain, the folks at WSB wanted to take one more stab at that Marconi Award. This year—2012—was to be my last in radio. It was the Year of Talking Dangerously! The theme throughout the year was "What are they going to do? *Fire me?*"

Maybe, just maybe, that Marconi was in reach. So they submitted the forms and, once again, I was nominated. Thanks, but no thanks. I was not going to make another wild goose chase to an NAB convention and yet another awards ceremony.

"But no!" they said. "We have a good feeling about this one! You're going to win!"

Right. But since the convention was in Dallas, and my brother lives in Dallas, I decided I could combine a family visit with just one more NBA dinner. No harm in that.

Sooooooo... I went.

I would like to congratulate sports talk dude Dan Patrick on receiving the Marconi for 2012 Network/Syndicated Talk Show Host of the year. Well deserved, Dan. Seriously. I mean it. Honestly.

In fact, I'm going to send you an autographed copy of this book. Well, if it wasn't an eBook I would.

Really.

At this point, I should apologize to Gordon Scott, the president of the National Association of Broadcasters. As The Queen and I were returning to our room, we encountered him in the elevator.

"Did you enjoy the dinner?" he asked?

I replied, "Not particularly."

OK, so I was disappointed. I didn't have to be a butthole about it. Actually, the dessert was pretty good.

I have the National Radio Hall of Fame going for me and, on top of that, no more NAB conventions. They can still use my initials, however.

I have no problem. Radio people are a special breed and there's no doubt I've enjoyed every minute of my 42 years working with these folks.

Sure beats the hell out of practicing law.

TALKMASTER'S TRUTHS

You can't spend all this time on the air pontificating to the masses and not come up with some basic truths that you fall back on—or share—with the listeners from time to time.

Some are immediately accepted as worthy and correct by most of the listeners. Some are rejected as complete and utter nonsense.

Some I came up with on my own; some I shamelessly stole from others.

At any rate, I present those that I can actually remember to you for your consideration.

These are the Talkmaster's Truths:

- The greatest status symbol anyone can ever have is a long-term marriage. You can't buy one—nor can you inherit one. The only path is to work for one, remembering that marriage is a 60/40 proposition. You give 60 percent and take 40 percent.
- When someone asks you how long you've been married, it's

always best for the guy to count from "I do" and not from "I did."

- The rich keep getting richer, because they keep doing the things that made them rich. Ditto for the poor.

- Barring physical or mental disaster, you are where you are today, materially and emotionally, due only to the combined effect of the choices you have made up to this point in your life. You always have the power of choice. How you use it will determine your future.

- I have never truly enjoyed a meal at a gourmet restaurant. Too long, too expensive, not enough food.

- Never eat anything that still has its eyes. Never eat anything that looks like it used to be something. Don't eat blue or white food.

- Never ask a women when she's due, unless you can actually see a little tiny body part starting to emerge from her body into the light of day.

- Every atheist prays that he's wrong when the end comes.

- Nobody can offend you without your permission.

- Why do fat women often have ankle tats? That's to draw attention to the only part of their body that looks somewhat normal.

- Working a 40-hour week isn't going to make you a success. Commute in the dark.

- A talk-radio caller who begins with "long-time listener, first-time caller" will NEVER have anything interesting to say beyond those six words.

- If you do not have the plumbing necessary to become pregnant, the world would appreciate it if you would just shut the hell up about abortion.

- Loud pipes do not save lives. They only piss people off and help to create a bad image for the rest of us on motorcycles out there.

- Motorcycles with loud pipes constantly have to be revved up at intersections. Motorcycles with normal, quiet exhaust systems can idle at a stoplight perfectly well.

- If your boyfriend or husband puts you on the back of a motorcycle without a helmet, he does NOT love you. You are merely a trophy that he will replace once your brains get scattered on the highway.

- Tattoos are a permanent reminder of an often-temporary emotion.

- A tattoo on your neck or face, no matter what the image or words, actually says, "I'm an idiot. Don't hire me."

- We have *exactly* the type of voters we have in this country today that our government schools were designed to create.

- People who don't know what they don't know are often exponentially more dangerous than people who know things that ain't so.

- "African-American" is a statement of origin, not a racial identification. If Ernie Els and Charlize Theron become U.S. citizens, they will be African-Americans.

- Buicks are incapable of traveling out of the left lane on a multi-lane highway and cannot exceed speeds of 35 miles per hour.

- I am at a loss to explain why anyone would voluntarily live and work where there is a state income tax. We are so mobile now that there are almost no excuses left for that behavior.

- Liberals think in terms of group identity. Conservatives think in terms of individuals. To a liberal, your group identity comes first—thus, the emphasis on "diversity."

- State licensing boards exist to protect various professions from competition, not to protect the consumers.

- Talk show hosts hang up on virtually *all* callers. If we allowed a caller to talk until they were finished and said goodbye, we would take only one—maybe two—callers per hour.

- The bottom of the college-bound high school class will major in education. The bottom of the graduate-school-bound college class will also major in education. Yes, there are exceptions, but people with graduate degrees in education are generally the dregs of the dregs of the dregs. That goes a long way in explaining our government schools.

- If you doubt my last point, let me show you the report card signed by a Clayton County, Georgia teacher with the handwritten notation, "Johnny are learning to get along with his pears."

- They are government schools, not public schools. The facilities are owned by the government and located on government land. The employees, from administrators to educators to janitors, are government employees. The curriculum is determined by government, as are all rules and regulations pertaining to the operation of these schools. They're <u>government</u> schools. Deal with it.

- With respect to flying your own airplane, it is always a lot better to be down here wishing you were up there than to be up there wishing you were down here.

- Grandparents get along so well with their grandchildren, because they share a common enemy.

- Parents should set aside enough money to pay for flying lessons for every teenager before they head off to college—just enough lessons to get them to the point they take off and land a few times alone—no instructor. The self-confidence that comes with that solo flight will serve them well the rest of their lives.

- If your teenager uses the word "like" in every sentence three or four times, forget the flying lessons. Tower controllers don't react well to "Peachtree Tower, this is, like, N134AP, and I'm, like, somewhere, like, north of the, like, airport near, like, the mall, and, like, I'm, like, coming in for a, like, landing." The controller will send your kid toward the mountains and hope he or she runs out of fuel.

- The driving age should be increased to 18. Simple as that.

- The driving-skills test for first-time driver's licenses should be designed to be so difficult that, without extensive training, you are almost guaranteed to fail it. Charge $200 for the test. That way, you can hire competent examiners. If you can't afford the $200, you don't need to be driving, anyway.

- Studies have shown that the safest drivers on expressways and freeways are those who are driving faster than the flow of traffic. It's those driving slower than the flow of traffic that cause the most accidents.
- When a law enforcement officer gives you a speeding ticket, he should change the patch on his uniform to read "Tax Collector."
- A Florida concealed weapons permit is more widely accepted than one issued in Georgia. That's because Florida requires training. Don't get your license in a state that does not require training and think that you can safely carry a weapon in public.
- The louder the radio commercial, the dumber the advertiser thinks his target customers are. Prime example: car commercials
- Perhaps the award for most idiotic statement ever made by a politician should go to South Dakota Democrat (of course) Senator Tom Daschle when he argued for turning all airport security over to the federal government by saying, "You don't professionalize unless you federalize." The TSA belongs to Tom Daschle.
- Referencing the last point, an argument could be made for statements made by 2012 Republican Senate candidates Todd Aiken and Richard Mourdock.
- I lived in a mobile home for a while in college. My wife and I also lived in a trailer for a while. I can, therefore, say what I damned well please about trailer trash.
- When you ride a motorcycle, wear road gear even in hot weather. You would much rather sweat than bleed. Dress for the slide, not the ride.
- When I started practicing law in 1977, it could be described as a profession. Today, it is more accurate to describe it as a trade.
- Hardwood floors in a law office are not a good idea. Corpu-

lent secretaries who insist on wearing spiked heels because it makes their bongo-sized legs look good will wear ruts from their desks to the copy machines and your clients will think they've just seen a water buffalo trail.

- Unless you're dealing with a true specialty, never hire a lawyer who advertises.
- The fancier the Mexican restaurant, the worse the food.
- The fuller the bra... the emptier the head... oh, just never mind.
- The most widespread form of child abuse in America is the act of sending your child to the government to be educated.
- The absolutely all-time greatest article ever written for any magazine, anywhere, at any time in our history, was *"Foreigners Around the World,"* written decades ago by P.J. O'Rourke for *National Lampoon Magazine.* If you pulled that article out today and read it in front of more than three people, you most certainly would be physically attacked, at best, and shot, at worst. But it's so funny that it is worth a try.
- The demise of our Republic will one day be blamed on our idiotic determination to allow every citizen to vote. So many are simply not intellectually qualified to cast a ballot. This is insanity.
- For the most part, the government school systems in most urban areas are little more than training academies for future government employees.
- Whether you think you can, or you can't, you're right.
- "Tough times don't last. Tough people do." (Rev. Robert Schuller)
- People who believe in a government-designed economy deride people who believe that God had a hand in designing our universe. Now just how stupid is that?
- I have not made a spelling error when I use the word "ignoranus."
- There is no reasonable excuse for hiring a smoker, except to serve as a bad example for the rest of your employees.

- The smoker's leper colonies outside of the workplace should be located near fire ant mounds.
- If you visit Hawaii, spend as little time in Waikiki as possible.
- Ebonics? That black dialect that prim and proper speakers of the English Language like to deride? Well, know this. The style of speech we like to refer to as Ebonics actually originated in Southern England before the Declaration of Independence was even signed.
- The most versatile word in the English language is the so-called "F-bomb." We need to get over our insane prudishness and put this word to its most effective usages.
- The sooner young black males learn that they are not going to be professional basketball players, the better off they will be and the greater their chances for success in life.
- "May I have the check please?" does *not* mean "Would you please clean off the table and then bring me the check?" You can clean up after I leave.
- I wholeheartedly approve of the death penalty. What's more, murderers should die the same way their victims did. For rape followed by murder, there is no shortage of bad boys in prison who would be all too happy to play a role in administering the just punishment.
- The ratings systems used to rate major market radio stations are horribly flawed. They weigh black listenership more heavily than is realistic in order to avoid problems with race pimps like Al Sharpton and Jesse Jackson. I'm not supposed to tell you this.
- Newspapers are dying. That's sad. An American who doesn't read a newspaper everyday is simply occupying space.
- When you see a lumbering lardass with a relatively normal husband, the odds are 95 to 1 that she didn't look like that when he married her—and the odds are 99 to 1 that he's not happy with Miss Double-Your-Fun's post-marriage appearance.
- "Racist" is the most overused and misunderstood word in our

modern language. It means absolutely nothing any more, except that the person using the word is an imbecile. Google "Semantic Saturation."

- Grammar Nazis—people who just love to tell people that it's "you're" not "your"—have very few friends and are generally terribly boring.
- Never trust people who don't like dogs or people that dogs clearly don't like.
- If you're really stopped up, get into an airplane above a 1000-foot overcast. That's the greatest laxative in the world.
- If *Fox News Channel* required its female anchors to wear slacks and loose-fitting blouses, their ratings would immediately drop by at least half.
- When it is time for me to make my last flight as pilot-in-command of a small airplane, I'm going to fly my Super Decathlon to Page Arizona. I will then, after a good night's sleep, fly over the Glen Canyon Dam and then right down the Grand Canyon just 50 feet above the Colorado River. I know where the bridges and cables are. I will then pull up, fly over the rim to the Bar 10 Ranch, land on their runway, leave my license in the airplane and walk away with a huge smile on my face.

It's painfully obvious to me at this point that I could go on for dozens of pages with this, but I need to move on and get this book up for you to download and enjoy.

So, for more of the *World According to Boortz,* just be sure to follow me on Twitter (@talkmaster) and check my blog on Boortz.com.

SOMETIMES IT REALLY SUCKS BEING RIGHT

… and I usually am, so I know what I'm talking about here, and boy did I call this one.

What did I get right?

The 2012 presidential election—that epic contest between Barack Obama and Mitt Romney.

In the final days leading up to the actual vote, I had various guests on the air who were promising—guaranteeing—that Romney was going to win this thing.

Oh yeah! It was going to be a landslide! According to them, Romney was going to get more than 330 electoral votes.

Noted cheapskate Clark Howard bet me that the Republicans were going to not only retain control of the House, but they were going to also take control of the Senate and the White House! *This was a slam-dunk!* The U-Haul for Obama's trip back to Chicago was already reserved.

Bolshoi.

I was having none of it. Through all this whistling past the graveyard, I was on the air telling my listeners that Obama was going to win.

Few agreed with me—and I can't think of one single prominent radio talk show host that agreed with my point of view.

Why was I certain of an Obama victory? Three statistics:

1. 49.1%   That's the percentage of American households in which at least one member is receiving a government check. Not Social Security or Medicare—*a government HANDOUT check.* These people will vote to keep those checks coming, and perhaps to get some more.

2. 40.7%   The percentage of babies born to single women. These are Obama voters. They're looking for someone else to pay the cost of raising their children. They want Obama to be their Sugardaddy.

3. 60%   And there you have the percentage of households that get more from the federal government in the form of various entitlement checks than they pay to the government in the form of taxes. They surely can be expected to keep it that way.

Now, try to overcome *that*!

Remember the *10 Commandments*? You do—in spite of everything that the government and our courts have done to bury them? Well, pardon me, but I did a little rewrite to one of them:

"Thou shalt not steal. Except by majority vote."

Actually Gary North said that. He's a historian. And though I've yet to see North weigh in on the 2012 presidential election, that pretty much explains what has happened.

So many people have been credited with so many different quotations regarding what happens when people figure out they can use their votes to take stuff away from other people.

Some of those quotes, like the one attributed to Alexander

Tytler, are false. Others, like those attributed to Thomas Jefferson, can be verified. The quotes, whether accurately attributed or not, are true. They make a valid point.

Face it—this was a "gimme election." A huge percentage of the voters on the winning side went to the polls with one thought in mind: Which one of these candidates is going to give me the most stuff? They have no thoughts on foreign relations, how to grow the economy, how to pay off our debt, how to ensure a prosperous future for our children.

Their thoughts were focused on how much money the government will take away from productive Americans and give to *them*.

For many, the realty has not yet sunk in.

It is almost impossible to believe that the voters actually passed up someone with the successes and abilities of Mitt Romney for the demonstrated failures of Barack Obama.

But *gimme, gimme, gimme* pretty much explains it.

Well, OK, there are reports that the Republicans just didn't do a good job getting their voters to the polls. Some have said that the problem was evangelicals who just wouldn't go to the polls to vote for a Mormon.

Great. Just great. Intolerant religious bigots strike again.

I'm afraid that this country is in decline. How can you look at the reelection of a complete failure like Barack Obama any other way?

How do we recover? How do we reverse the trend? Truthfully, I'm not sure we can—but freedom and liberty are always worth the effort.

We must try.

REPUBLICAN PARTY ... LET ME HELP YOU OUT

The tragic election loss? It boils down to this—and, trust me, this is going to make some of you as mad as hornets.

That's why I put it at the end of the book.

At least before you got here, you learned a little more about me and had a bit of fun. I could fill these remaining pages with more fun—but I'm writing just after a hideous loss for America, so I'm going to vent.

You don't like it? Close the book and go clean something.

Let's look backward: I remember the morning after the 1994 Congressional elections. Do you? Clinton had been president for two years. HillaryCare was on the table. Clinton was toying with the idea of levying a one-time 15% tax on the outstanding balance in every American's IRA, 401K or pension plan to "shore up Social Security."

The voters had had enough, and Clinton woke up to a Republican Congress and Senate. Two months later, in his State of the Union address, Clinton said, "The era of big government is over."

The Republicans used their newfound strength to throw a roadblock in front of Clinton's spending plans, and to force him into accepting (and later claiming credit for) welfare reform. Some talk show hosts were saying that we need to keep some liberals around for scientific study and the amusement of our children in zoos.

Not me.

I was warning my listeners that the Democrats would come back. It could take years, but they would come back. And when they did come back—when they finally gained control of the machinery of the federal legislative process again—they would work with blinding speed to make as many Americans dependent as quickly as possible.

Well, they did, indeed, come back—four years ago, with the election of Barack Obama and a Democrat Senate and House.

And they began the push to do exactly what I said they would do. They worked feverishly to expand government dependency. Welfare vastly expanded. Welfare work rules relaxed.[50] Food stamp use exploded.[51] And don't forget ObamaCare.

It's not going to get better. The welfare state will expand even more. The 49.1 percent of Americans mentioned above will grow to well over 50 percent by the next election. The 60 percent of American households who get more unearned money from the government every year than they pay in taxes—that number will expand as well.

The numbers on food stamps and Social Security disability will expand, and ObamaCare will create still another dependent demographic: Government health-care dependents. By 2016, the Democrats will have achieved their decades-long dream of being

[50]Can you believe that, under welfare work rules established by Obama, writing in your diary counts as work? So does walking your neighbor's dog. Picking your nose? No. Your neighbor's nose? Possibly!

[51]For every person who found a job during the first four years of Obama's rule, 75 people were approved for food stamps.

able to go into an election battle saying, "If you vote for the Republicans, they are going to take away your medical care."

The argument could be made that this was our last chance. This election. 2012.

Our LAST chance—and we blew it.

Turning this country back toward freedom, economic liberty and self reliance will be an even tougher task in the midterm elections of 2014, and probably impossible in 2016. By 2016, even more Americans will realize that they can use the ballot as a weapon—a legal weapon—to do something that would put them in jail if they did it with a gun. That is take someone else's money.

Game. Set. Match.

Those people cheering this Obama victory have no real idea what was going on in the minds of business owners across America after the election. Some were making plans to close less-profitable locations and lay off employees. Some businessmen were shelving plans for expansion and more hiring, deciding that it would be better to take their money and put it where it will be safe from the coming tax increases.

Other businessmen were preparing to fire some employees and reduce others to part-time status in order to stay below the employee threshold on ObamaCare.

People who voted for Obama were, in many instances, out of a job by the end of the week, because their election wishes came true. Newspapers and the Internet were full of stories of business owners trimming their workforces to prepare for ObamaCare now that repeal was off the table.

Here's an interesting dynamic that the low-information voters who put Obama over the top will not be able to grasp: As businesses cut back on employees, and as they move more employees to a part-time status in order to escape the mandates of ObamaCare and other government regulations, the employees who will suffer—the employees who will lose their jobs or be relegated to part-time status with lower pay—will be the less capable, less educated employees who voted for Obama for a second term.

They will never understand that their job situation has become more tenuous because of the vote they cast. They simply aren't intelligent enough to understand that.

They've done this to themselves, but they are too ignorant to realize it.

Are you wondering what the wonderful low-information voters brought us with their reelection of Obama?

Here, let me drop a few reminders. This is what's on the way:

- Higher taxes on productive Americans, of course. Exit polls showed that most voters want this. Obama's class warfare tactics worked like a charm.
- Labor unions will renew their push for card-check—unionization by intimidation.
- The United Nations will gain in strength and exercise more power over Americans. Look for restrictions of American's Second Amendment rights rather quickly.
- Taxes on jobs producing small businessmen will almost certainly go up.
- Obama will issue a call for another multi-billion-dollar stimulus bill that will do nothing other than reward cronies and campaign contributors.
- Doctors who have been in practice for many years will be closing up shop. They know what a nightmare ObamaCare is going to be for their patients, and they want no part of it. My doctor in Atlanta called me the day after the election to tell me he was retiring—effective immediately.
- The EPA will unleash a flood of new "clean air" regulations that will all but destroy the coal industry and bring huge increases in the cost of energy.
- Democrats will start talking about a scheme to levy a tax against retirement and pension funds on the premise that it is not fair some people are going to have a comfortable retirement, while others will have to shove shopping carts at customers entering Wal-Mart.
- The push for ETIs will return—Economically Targeted Invest-

ments. This means that the government will tell you where you can and cannot invest your qualified retirement (401K, IRA) funds. The purpose will be to force you to invest these funds in "union-friendly" (i.e., unionized) companies.

- Democrats will develop schemes to punish states with Right-To-Work laws in an attempt to force more Americans into joining unions in order to work.
- Democrats will attack talk radio with community advisory boards and shorter license renewal periods. Syndicated talk radio may be a thing of the past in four years—except for Clark Howard, of course.

I have a message to the Republican Party, or what's left of it.

The Republican Party needs an exorcism.

It needs to rid itself of these abortocentrist nutcases—usually men—who are chasing away voters, particularly women. This is about as clearly as I can say it: Abortion is NEVER going to be illegal. *Get over it!* The sooner you come to terms with this, the sooner you will be able to regain credibility with the voters.

Your boys Todd Aiken, Richard Mourdock and John Koster chased away millions of female voters with their idiotic remarks about abortion and they cost us two seats in the Senate.

How bad was it?

Romney carried Mourdock's home county in Indiana! His opponent, Joe Donnelly, was the first Democrat to win a statewide race in Indiana in more than a decade!

Are you listening, Republicans? Mourdock was a shoo-in! Then he opened his yap about abortion, and women went screaming for the exits. What did he say? Well, simply put, the message to women was that if you've been raped, don't worry your pretty little selves over whether or not you might be pregnant because, if you are, it is, after all, a gift from God!

Here's the problem, dear GOP leaders: Read this quote from Wayne Parke. He's the Chairman of the Vanderburgh County Republican Party. That's Mourdock's home county—the one he lost:

"I was quite surprised and disappointed that Mourdock didn't carry his own county. But it's an indication that everything you say is so important and that debate comment he made just turned out to be disastrous..."

Duhhhhhhh! Really?

You've learned that lesson now, have you, Mr. Parke? Could you please send some memos to the Republican National Headquarters? Who knows, if you and the GOP leaders had figured this out months ago, and if the word had gone out that GOP candidates needed to shut the hell up about abortion, maybe things would look quite a bit different today.

The same goes for gay marriage.

If you can make the case that a married gay couple living down the street from you, or across town for that matter, is going to have any negative impact on your own life, then I would say that we need to have a debate on the subject. Nobody has shown me that, yet, so how about getting your GOP noses out of other people's bedrooms?

I've been on the air for years and never in my 42 years of talk radio has anyone been able to tell me how Joe and Steve living down the block in wedded bliss will have *any* impact on his or her life. Come into the 21st century with me on this one and just leave the issue the hell alone.

If you're so determined to defend the institution of marriage—the concept of committed couples living together in a dedicated relationship—then why don't you turn your attention to Hollywood? Forget about demonizing a gay couple that is every bit as much in love and committed as you are to your spouse. Aim your derision on the Hollywood crowd that looks at marriage as not much more than a new car—something to be traded in on a new model in two years—or two months.

And when it comes to immigration, rounding up all the Mexicans in this country and sending them back to Mexico is never, ever going to happen.

Do you hear that? It *isn't* going to happen!

Does it occur to you that these people come here because they *want* to work? Do you really have such a huge problem with aspirational people? So come up with a reasonable policy on immigration reform, and lock down the borders.

No problem with that.

But give up this asinine idea that those already here—those who have been here for years—are going to be loaded into railroad cars and sent back to Mexico. Do you really want that? Do you really want to depend on those Americans who would rather spend their days hanging around convenience stores scratching goo off lottery tickets than put in an honest day's work? Do you really want to pay $16 for a BLT?

Yeah, that's right. Scare the folks with the actual work ethic away while pampering the moochers and leaches.

Yeah, that works.

What do you think a Hispanic American citizen thinks when he sees a political party dedicate itself to the cause of taking a young female college student—a young lady who has lived here since her parents brought her here illegally when she was 3—and deporting her to a country she has never known?

Do you think it's likely that Hispanic citizen is going to vote for your candidate? Tell me how that works.

Stop crying in your beer and listen up. America is going to suffer another four years under Obama because of YOU. The Republican Party blew this one—big time. Abortion—gay marriage—immigration reform. The perfect electoral storm, and you couldn't have played it any worse. What's more, you couldn't even get your base out to vote.

Leave these issues alone! *Drop them!* If the GOP cannot turn loose of this mindless social conservatism, then you will be relegated to second-class status (politically speaking) for the remaining days of this Republic, which may not be all that many.

The Republican Party, as it currently stands, needs to die. Like a phoenix, it needs to burst into flames and, from its ashes, rebuild into a party focused on:

- Limited government
- Tax reform
- A strong military
- The rule of law
- Reducing regulations
- Promoting capitalism—especially small businesses
- Restoring self-reliance
- Honoring the Constitution

Did you see abortion or gay marriage on that list? Didn't think so.

The Republicans need to become more Libertarian and less religiously authoritarian or the Party is dead. It's amazing that these social conservatives have managed to screw this country they claim to love so much by handing Democrats victories, thanks to these social issues.

THANK YOU

Someone (my editor—GAWD, can she crack the whip or what?) told me that the book ended rather suddenly. It was like I signed off at the end of the show and just said, "We won't be back."

Well, I *will* be back, and this isn't the end of the show—just a shift in the methodology. I'll be doing daily commentaries on *WSB* and any other station that will have me. I'll be substituting for Herman Cain and any other talk show host who will invite me. I'll be making speeches to anyone who wants their convention or meeting disrupted. I'll be blogging on Boortz.com and raising hell on Twitter (@talkmaster).

If you really wanna, you can get your share of me.

But perhaps a better way to close out this book would be to thank some folks—and that includes a few who might not be expecting a thank you.

Ahhhh, where to start? I've already thanked my family for putting up with this elsewhere in the book, so the only other logical place to start would be with my listeners—and the callers.

Here's something you may not know, and the research is a few years old on this. The numbers may have changed, but I rather doubt it. Only about 1 to 1½ percent of the people who listen to talk radio will ever try to call the show. Chances are that, if you're a listener, you've never tried to call.

The callers are important, to be sure, but my best calculation is that I've only taken somewhere from 190,000 to 210,000 phone calls in my 42 years of talk radio. Considering that most of these people—at least half—are repeat callers, that would mean that about 95,000 to 105,000 listeners have called in. The experts say I have around six million people listening, so do the math and you'll see it comes out pretty close.

The callers have been great, no doubt. Some have educated me. Others have amused me. And, of course, some have infuriated me. But they were listening, and they cared enough about something, even if it was only a desire to insult me, to make that call and wait on line.

To all of you, THANK YOU!

A special thanks, however, goes to the listeners. There cannot possibly be one listener—well, one long-time listener anyway—that I haven't infuriated or offended[52] in some way or another over the years. Mad, ticked off, outraged, pleased, amused, affirmed—I guess the listeners went through all of this.

My one hope and constant goal, though, was to entertain.

I gotta admit, some of the listeners have been a real source of constant amusement for us and our advertisers. Let me tell you about some of them.

First, there's the "I'm never going to listen to you, again" (IN-GTLTYA) crowd. I can't even guess the number of times I've received emails or letters from people who deliver this "I'm never going to listen to you, again" line. Usually, it's after I've expressed my intemperate thoughts on what are generally referred to as social issues. I'm a Libertarian. That pretty much means I believe the government should leave people alone. Some listeners aren't wired that way, and there's no doubt about it: A few Libertarian thoughts on social issues can bring out the "I'm never going to listen to you, again" crowd in a flash.

OK, for the INGTLTYA crowd, know this: At best, talk radio pulls in about 15-17 percent of the people listening to a radio in any one broadcast market at any one particular moment. This means that you have now joined the majority! Aren't you happy and thrilled? This is *just* where you belong! With the majority! Nothing unique or special about you! *No sireeee!*

Besides, you know and we know that you are going to be listening to my show the very next day, just as you always have—if for no other reason than to find something else about which you can complain. Really, if every single one of the INGTLTYA crowd had actually stopped listening to my show, I would have been off the air

[52]OH! You were offfffffffended? Like I care. Nobody can offend you without your permission. It was your problem, not mine. Now there's a painful truth you need to accept.

many moons ago for lack of an audience.

So to you, I say THANK YOU! I know I made you madder than hell, and you were probably serious—for a minute or two—about never listening again. But I know you stayed. Even better, I know you stayed, because you enjoyed what I was doing. Really... *thank you*! You were some of my most loyal listeners of all.

And for those who wrote complaint mail and called the boss to demand that I be fired, killed, disemboweled, neutered, or doused in kerosene and torched, THANK YOU! Really! Thanks!

You see, for a period of time, the Boortz Show staff actually got a small bonus every time an irate listener managed to get through the gauntlet to the boss. Time after time, I was told that management would get nervous when the complaint letters and calls *stopped*!

If nobody is complaining, nobody is listening.

So for the listeners who provided the cash stash from which Belinda, Royal, Cristina and I occasionally bought lunch and adult beverages, a big THANK YOU!

For a while—about two years—I wrote a weekly column for *The Atlanta Journal-Constitution*. After I had been writing for about six months or so, the *WSB* station manager, Marc Morgan, received a call from one of the suits at the newspaper.

"Marc. We're having a problem with Boortz's column."

"What's that?"

"We're getting complaints."

"How many complaints have you received?"

"Oh, about two."

Morgan broke down laughing.

"Two? You've only received two complaints? Let me tell you something. If we had received only two complaints about Boortz during the first six months he was on the air here, he never would have made it to the seventh month."

Oh well, difference in management style, I guess. The *AJC* finally fired me from my columnist position.

Damn. *Fired, again.*

Writing the column really was a royal pain so, to the cowering editors at the *AJC*, THANK YOU!

There was one type of complainer that particularly amused me. These were the people who would call my advertisers to say that they would never do business with them, because they sponsored the *Boortz Show*.

Yeah, right.

There's one particular Atlanta institution that I've been plugging for nearly 40 years: Bennie's Shoes. These folks first opened for business 100 years ago and, when it comes to shoe repair and great prices on new shoes, they can't be beat. Louie Shemaria, the Bennie's patriarch, loves to tell the story of a man who came into his store one day and bought a few hundred dollars' worth of new shoes.

"How did you hear about us?"

"*The Neal Boortz Show*."

"Oh! Do you like Neal?"

"Hell no! I can't stand the sonovabitch."

"Well, excuse me sir for asking but, if you can't stand Neal, why are you buying shoes from us?"

"Because he said you were great, and I believe everything that sorry bastard says on the radio."

True story. Ask Louie.

That is one of the finest endorsements of my endorsement advertising impact I have received in my 42 years on the air. So, sir, whoever you are and wherever you may be, THANK YOU.

I think I'll use this as a springboard for a little dissertation of endorsing sponsors. Actually, I think other talk show hosts and radio personalities might benefit from what I have to say here.

Only one time in my career did I ever endorse a product or service on the local radio station that I did not personally own or use. That one time was when I endorsed Steinway Pianos. I knew they were the best, and I had always wanted to play a piano. Thought maybe they would give me one, but no such luck. Didn't work out that way.

Still don't know how to play anything but Chopsticks.

The listeners came to trust that what I told them about a local advertiser came from personal experience and could be relied upon. That helped the sales weasels get out there and close the deal.

Treat your listeners right, and they'll return the favor with loyalty. So to the listeners who made a point of shopping with my endorsement advertisers, THANK YOU!

Let's move on to the listeners of the, let's say, disgruntled[53] variety. I just *loved* it when these listeners would call an advertiser to tell them how disgusting it was that they were advertising on my show.

"Mr. So-and-so! I just want you to know that I was going to be coming over to your computer store with about 10 friends tomorrow to buy new computers, but now we're going to take our business somewhere else, because you advertise on the *Neal Boortz Show*!"

Yeah! *Sure* you were! In fact, you were going to charter a bus to bring your whole freaking neighborhood over to buy a computer – a car – a diamond engagement ring – some furniture – office supplies – a new garage door – pest control services – *whatever*! You were all coming over, and now you're not.

Uh huh! *You bet*!

My advertisers and I would have a good laugh talking about and listening to recordings of these calls. Somehow, in spite of all those neighborhoods that turned their charter busses around, these businesses thrived. When the advertising stopped, they suffered. And so it goes.

So to the advertisers who withstood the irate calls and letters— calls and letters I told them would come their way when they first signed up to advertise—all these years, I've been working for YOU.

---

[53]Just a thought here, but have you ever given any thought to the word "disgruntled?" I can't help but wonder where it came from. After all, have you ever been gruntled? Doesn't there have to be a gruntled if there is a disgruntled? Were you ever gruntled with a meal? A Broadway show? A fling in the hay?

Here's another big THANK YOU.

To all the stations who didn't take my show because it was "Southern," I want you to know that, oddly enough, you may well have done me a favor. My career has pretty much been as a back bencher. Rush and Sean were out there with the tens of millions of listeners, so the leftist media pretty much focused on them.

Oh, to be sure, I got my share of attention every once in a while. *The FairTax Book* resulted in a publicity orgy and even took me to Washington D.C. to testify before a Senate Subcommittee. But, for the most part, I've been yapping away in the background out of the leftist crosshairs.

So I didn't have more listeners! So what! Most people don't drive Mercedes Benz automobiles, either. I subscribe to the theory that the nail that sticks out the farthest gets pounded down first. Well, my nail didn't stick out quite so far as the big guys. Looks like I'm going to make good my escape without having been pounded into the ground.

To the stations that sacrificed great ratings by not taking this "Southern show," THANK YOU! You saved me from getting too big for my britches.

To Rush and Sean, THANK YOU for taking the brunt while I was sitting back, raising absolute hell and remaining relatively unscathed.

Okay, I realize that maybe I've been just a bit snarky here in this last chapter. (Trust me—my editor, who tries to protect me from myself, beat me up about it.)

I've had 42 years to perfect snarky, to raise it to an art form. We'll just call this the artist's final brush strokes.

But in all sincerity, to the fans and detractors alike, radio station general managers, program directors, sales staffs and advertisers who have carried my show and to those of you who invited me into your communities to commiserate with your local listeners, I extend a genuine, heartfelt *thank you.*

You helped me run from the law. You helped me escape the grueling and tension-filled life of an attorney and settle into the always-fun job of hosting a talk show. I would recommend this profession to everyone. Sadly, there's just not enough room for all y'all. (That Southern thing, again).

It seemed that, one way or another, I was going to end up behind that talk radio microphone.

It was meant to be.

Once I got there you—all of you—got behind me and we had ourselves one helluva ride, didn't we?

What was that the Terminator said?

Oh yeah... *I'll be back.*

AFTERWORD

OK. That's about it.

Before we sign off, a few final thanks. There is no way I can mention and thank everyone who had a part in my talk radio career, but there are some who stand out.

I must start, of course, with my wife, Donna, and our daughter, Laura. Trust me, this hasn't been easy for them. Donna has NEVER listened to my show. That has actually been a blessing, because I'm sure she would not have approved of the way I treated some of the callers. Though they weren't listeners, my wife and daughter had to endure years of strangers, and sometimes friends, verbally assaulting them with "Did you hear what your husband said today?" or "What does Neal think about such-and-such?" These two put up with a lot. I love them both dearly.

I don't want this to turn into a name-a-thon, but there are some people who will always be a part of my life. There's Royal Marshall, of course. Even though he passed away two years ago, he's still there, trying to keep me somewhat calmed down and on the right path.

Belinda Skelton has been my producer and office wife for 18 years. She likes to tell people that we had the fights without the makeup sex. Belinda is on Twitter at @WSBelinda. I will do all that I can to keep Belinda in my life for the years to come.

The same goes for Cristina. That's Cristina Michelle Gonzalez-Schaeffer. Cuban—100 percent—and possibly the smartest young lady I've ever met. But *ohhhhh* does she have the hang-ups. Don't ever touch her with your foot. Not without earplugs.

Then there's Marc Morgan. He rescued me from the evil Jacor and finally made broadcasting a completely fun experience.

And there's Bugsy! That's Greg Moceri, one of the greatest talk radio brains out there. He taught me how to increase ratings without adding listeners. When I did what he told me to do, the bonus money rolled in. When I didn't, I had to beg the wife for spending money.

Special thanks to Cheryl Lewis—my editor. She's amazing. She was once married to a talk show host, so she has an idea how I think. She is now dedicated to helping people in need, and this book was edited between sprints to New Orleans and New Jersey to help hurricane and storm victims, Haiti to help earthquake victims, and Atlanta to keep her husband and kids on the straight and narrow. Cheryl is quite a writer herself. You can follow her on Twitter at @getaclewis or www.CherylLewis. com.

That's pretty much it, except for you, my listeners. For those of you who agreed with me all the time, some of the times, or never—but who listened, nonetheless—thanks for being there to afford me a wonderful career.

I can scarcely fathom how fortunate I am to have fallen into this job (sorry, Herb) and to have you folks out there listening, buying stuff from my advertisers, and responding to those pesky ratings surveys, so that I didn't have to go back to practicing law.

Soon (perhaps already, depending upon when you read this), I'm off somewhere on the BoortzBus, flying my Mooney to some small, out-of-the-way airport, or just trying to reach the green on number 13 in two.

If I get good at this watercolor thing, I'll have an art show and invite all of you.

Love you.
Mean it.
Neal.